ONE on ONE

THE BEST MEN'S MONOLOGUES

FOR THE 21ST CENTURY

ONE ON ONE

THE BEST MEN'S MONOLOGUES

FOR THE 21ST CENTURY

EDITED BY
JOYCE E. HENRY
REBECCA DUNN JAROFF
BOB SHUMAN

APPLAUSE THEATRE & CINEMA BOOKS
An Imprint of Hal Leonard Corporation
New York

Published in 2008 by Applause Theatre & Cinema Books
An Imprint of Hal Leonard Corporation
7777 West Bluemound Road
Milwaukee, WI 53213

Trade Book Division Editorial Offices
19 West 21st Street, New York, NY 10010

Printed in the United States of America

Book design by Kristina Rolander

Library of Congress Cataloging-in-Publication Data

One on one : the best men's monologues for the 21st century / edited by
Joyce E. Henry, Rebecca Dunn Jaroff, and Bob Shuman.
p. cm.
  ISBN 978-1-55783-701-1
  1. Monologues. 2. Acting–Auditions. 3. Men--Drama. 4. American
drama–21st century. I. Henry, Joyce E. II. Jaroff, Rebecca Dunn. III. Shuman,
Bob.

  PN2080.O56 2008
  808.82'45089286–dc22
                              2008039493

www.applausepub.com

CONTENTS

PART TWO: THE EXTENDED MONOLOGUE

EDITORS' NOTE

In some scenes there are other characters onstage or those who will be entering. To indicate this, we have included their speeches or stage directions in brackets. Do not disregard them; your responses provide important clues for your character.

In the table of contents, you will notice that certain speeches are designated by a specific ethnic identity, as determined by the playwright in the context of the whole play. However, most if not all of the monologues in this book are far more flexible and accessible to a broad range of actors and can be performed by any actor who is drawn to the material. The same is true about the flexibility of the age of designations.

Some speeches might be longer than are called for in your situation. Again, the material may provide important clues to your motivation and background, but you may need to cut some in the interest of time. Under certain circumstances it may be appropriate to inform the audience that the speech is abridged.

FOREWORD

As a Broadway casting director who has cast over seventy-five plays, television films and motion pictures, I have seen countless performed monologues. Some are memorable, but most are difficult to sit through, and some even painful. This book should help to make your audition memorable.

Choosing the appropriate monologue for an audition is crucial. Monologues are routinely required for most regional companies, Broadway and Off-Broadway companies, and admission to college theatre programs and to private acting classes. Most British directors prefer them to reading from the actual script. As an actor, you undoubtedly will be asked to perform a solo piece at some time, so choose carefully.

The most important tip I can provide you about performing a monologue successfully is to make a strong choice. It doesn't matter what choice it is — BUT it has to have one clear point of view. There's nothing worse than an actor who thinks he can show many facets of his talent in one reading. Can't be done. The audition becomes wishy-washy, neither fish nor fowl, and the auditors are left unimpressed. Unless otherwise suggested by your teacher in an acting class, be sure to select a monologue that is age appropriate and close to your persona. This is not the time to stretch.

Probably the biggest mistake actors make is choosing to perform an overly familiar piece. How many times can a stressed-out casting director listen to Tom's Act One long speech from *The Glass Menagerie*? Or Edmund speaking about his memorable days at sea in *A Long Day's Journey into Night*? The book you're looking at now can be a godsend, because all the speeches come from plays written since the year 2000. Some of the speeches are from well-known award-winning playwrights; others are from authors writing in regional theatres or Off-Broadway, but all offer fresh ideas and challenges to the actor. Chances are they will be totally unfamiliar or only partly familiar to the listeners and, even if recognized, will not be identified with Marlon Brando or Rip Torn.

If you do make a wrong choice, live with it and learn from it. I remember an actress who came in to audition for a Broadway play. She chose material that was not only wrong for the character for which she was auditioning, but also was 180 degrees away from her own personality. As she slogged through her choice, she sensed that the auditors were not responding, but she finished anyway. Then she let go. She swore, stamped her foot, in general made a great scene, and stalked out. Needless to say, she demonstrated that she would not be an asset to any company she worked with, and even if she had been brilliant they would not have hired her. It's okay to be disappointed in your audition, but wait until you leave the room before letting everyone know how you feel. Then go home and work on a speech more suited to your personality—and talent.

When the audition process works, it really works. I'll never forget Joe Morton's audition for a wonderful Broadway play titled *The Mighty Gents*. His monologue was telling a friend about a traumatic experience the character had had. We didn't know the monologue. It was totally unfamiliar. We thought he was telling a true story from his past. When we realized he had just gotten into his audition, we all were blown away. Needless to say, he got the job.

After you have chosen your speech, if at all possible, read the entire play, to make certain that your interpretation of the character is accurate. This may take an effort, as some of the plays here have been published, and some not, but if you like the author's work, you owe it to him or her to provide credit, so using a little actor's ingenuity, you can manage it.

Choose wisely, prepare well, and good luck—the theatre is always in need of good, hardworking and intelligent actors.

BARRY MOSS

Barry Moss is a partner in Hughes Moss Casting, responsible for casting over sixty Broadway plays and musicals, including *Nine*, *Titanic*, *Jekyll & Hyde*, and *A Tale of Two Cities*. The company also cast *The Cosby Show* on NBC-TV for nine years and "discovered" or, more accurately, gave first jobs to Tom Cruise, Adam Sandler, Ricky Schroeder, Raven-Symone, James Spader, Catherine Keener, Donna Murphy, Raul Esparza, Matthew McConaughey, and Frances McDormand, among others.

PART ONE

A WORLD OF MONOLOGUES

THE ADVENTURES OF NERVOUS-BOY (A PENNY DREADFUL)

BY JAMES COMTOIS

After a rather awkward evening at an avant-garde play and a boring party, the NERVOUS BOY, *a young man in his 20s, candidly expresses his feelings for Emily.*

SCENE
A New York bar

TIME
The present

NERVOUS BOY: I've . . . I mean . . . I just think you're so funny, and . . . smart, and . . . interesting . . . and beautiful. I just feel like I'm throwing myself at you, and . . . I'm sorry. I just . . . think you're wonderful. I've had feelings for you since we first met, and . . . I've been trying to snap out of it for the longest time, but . . . no. I love you. That is . . . I'm falling in love with you. I care about you. And I worry about you. I worry about your career and whether or not you're being exploited. I worry about your father. I care about what you want in life and I care about you getting it. It's just so many times we talk and I'm listening but part of me is terrified that you see the hearts in my eyes and . . . I just . . . think you're wonderful. And I love you. And . . . I'm sorry. (*Pause.*) I haven't been able to find a full-time job since I got laid off two years ago. I really don't know what I'm doing with my life and I'm kind of freaking out about it but I think I'm too lazy to really fix that problem and I get so sick of being lost in my thoughts and being by myself and I'm tired of being too scared to look at anyone in the eye anymore and I just love seeing you, Emily, and talking to you, because when I do I forget about all my anxieties for a short while and it feels like a giant weight has been lifted for a brief time and I'm not filled with guilt or self-loathing. . . . I just like . . . being with you. I feel like a real person. You know? And . . . I'm sorry. I just . . . I haven't felt like that in a while and I'm sorry and I'm rambling.

ALIENS, 3 MILES, TURN LEFT
BY STEPHEN A. SCHRUM

In his living room, cluttered with pizza boxes and other signs of bachelor living, a MAN *in his late 30s talks about his eerie close encounter with aliens in his backyard.*

SCENE
The living room

TIME
The present

MAN: And then, one night last spring, They came. I was just coming home from one of our poker nights, and it was pretty late. As I came up the driveway, I saw something out in the field. There was this weird greenish light. I didn't know what it could be, so I turned off the truck and drifted to a stop. I also pulled out my rifle I keep in the gun rack, and I snuck out to the field. And there I saw it.

Right then, I knew it was all true. I'd read about it in the *National Enquirer* and the *Weekly World News,* but here it was right in front of me. Space aliens. There were three of them, about four or five feet tall, with long arms and legs, wearing some strange clothes, with these funny helmets, that looked sorta familiar but

I couldn't quite figure it out. They were walking around outside their ship, picking up rocks and weeds and stuff, and checking them out with some kind of small box they had, just like on (*mispronounces*) *Star Track*. But they didn't see me; they just kept on doing what they were doing, and I just kept watching them moving around, picking up rocks and weeds and stuff.

After a couple of minutes, two of them walked over to the ship and start staring at some kind of crystal thing, and it starts turning purple. It was the weirdest thing, them just holding this big crystal and it starts glowing. This was kind of interesting, so I just kept watching them staring at this thing. Then all of a sudden, out of the corner of my right eye, I see that the third one is standing next to me, staring at me, and he's got some kind of little box pointed right at me. Hell, I don't know if it's a gun or what, so I take the butt of my rifle and I knock it out of his hands. But he doesn't do anything, he just stands there, staring at me with these big weird eyes. And then I hear footsteps, and I look over and the other two are running toward us, and the crystal's glowing brighter, and I figure I'm in some kind of deep shit now.

So I shot 'em. I shot all three of 'em. First I shot the two running at me, and then the third. I musta scared the crap out of him, 'cause he started singing, uh, some kind of high-pitched opera thing. It gave me the shivers! So I shot him too. Man, that was weird. It was easier than shooting deer. I just shot 'em.

So there I am, out in this field, with three dead aliens and an alien spaceship. And I'm trying to figure out what to do next. And then it hits me. I gotta hide this. I mean, I read these articles about when people call the government about crashed ships, and they come in and they take it all away and you can't even prove that it really happened. And everybody thinks you're nuts.

AN ALMOST HOLY PICTURE

BY HEATHER MCDONALD

SAMUEL GENTLE *is a groundskeeper for The Church of the Holy Comforter.* HE *is 49, has thinning hair, and wears glasses. His gardening clothes include a tattered tweed jacket, a straw hat, and a highly polished silver concha belt.*

SCENE
The grounds and a crypt in a cathedral, The Church of the Holy Comforter. Stained glass, soaring columns, some soft light coming through the darkness. Wind. Fallen leaves.

TIME
November

SAMUEL: At the age of 42, Miriam gave birth to a tiny girl child covered all over in a white-gold swirl of hair. The doctor (another one, not the fuckwad) held her high and said, "Lanugo." Lanugo? I'd only ever heard this word in relation to the garden. There is a climbing plant, a native to China, called "Clematis Lanuginosa." It's a dark green vine, and the undersurface of the leaf is covered with the softest grey wool. What did this have to do with my daughter?

When I suggested we call her Ariel since she seemed to me a tiny, shimmering angel, Miriam snorted (she does that sometimes — snorts) and said, "Humph, a misguided angel."

When I looked at this wrinkled cooing bird that was my daughter and held her tight little fists in my hands, my ribcage expanded to make room as my heart grew bigger. Her whole body shuddered with an intake of breath. A breath of heaven. And what I felt then was truer than what, for most of us, passes for love, because it was uncorrupted by love's hunger and fear of loss and damaging desperation. It was wide open and as big as all creation.

Miriam and Ariel stayed in the hospital for a week. Doctors and nurses conferred quietly on our daughter. Miriam requested books on the subject. My clearest memory of that week is of Miriam propped up in bed, nursing Ariel, and reading some enormous medical text. Whenever I came into the room, I was astonished to see a furry little creature rooting around at my wife's breast, and the sight of Miriam's fingers gently stroking the curls on Ariel's back caused my throat to swell and for a moment it was hard to swallow. Miriam read some paragraphs aloud from the textbooks, but I wasn't really listening. By the end of the week, she said, "It seems to me, Samuel, that we have something serious to deal with."

Lanugo is a mysterious and rare disease. Lanugo is a fine, silky hair that coats the face and body. The more technical name for our daughter's condition is Congenital Hypertrichosis Lanuginosa. It is a distressing disorder, usually hereditary, passed unknowingly from the opposite-sex parent, mother to son, father to daughter. The doctors know little about the cause. There are temporary measures, but no permanent treatment.

Our Ariel is covered with the lightest, golden down. In some light, she fairly shimmers. I think of her as our misguided angel.

AN ALMOST HOLY PICTURE
BY HEATHER MCDONALD

SAMUEL GENTLE, *50s, is invited to an art gallery where photographs are being displayed by a friend of the family.*

SCENE
Truro on Cape Cod

TIME
Summer

SAMUEL: I stepped into the gallery. It was a day of clear blue light, so it took a moment for my eyes to adjust. When they did, what I saw was this. Displayed on the walls of the Traynor Gallery were photographs of my 9-year-old daughter (covered in hair from her disease) taken by that wild child Angel Martinez. I know now what Ariel does between the hours of three and six. Something fierce in me lurched forward, blocking one photograph with my hands, trying to protect my daughter from the eyes of others. I remember how panicked I felt when I saw how many photographs there were. I staggered through the gallery pulling photographs from the walls, letting them smash to the ground behind me. Glass shattered. Ariel screamed. I called Angel Martinez "a foul creature." I gathered as many of the photographs as I could carry into my arms, hidden safely away, and I ran from the gallery.

I stopped visiting Mr. Martinez in the mornings and instead spent the time looking at these photographs.

Let me describe these for you now.

(HE *holds the packet of photographs. We should not see the actual photographs.*)

The first few are a series of Ariel swimming naked in the Bay, turning over in the water like a sleek, wet seal. There's another of her, in the woods, crouched, a small startled animal. And another where she's sitting on a white blanket eating blackberries. Her fingers and hands are stained, and the dark juice has dribbled down her chin and runs down her chest and stomach so that her body looks bruised and streaked with blood. There's one where she's wearing a large hat decorated with ribbons and feathers and plumes and she's sitting cross-legged in dungarees and grinning straight at the camera. In another one she's in the woods asleep, and I believe she really was asleep because her mouth is slightly open in the way it is when she sleeps. And someone's covered her body with twigs and branches and leaves.

There is this one photograph, though, that I must tell you about in greater detail. It is a study in contrasts, light and dark. I believe the term is chiaroscuro. Ariel is running up a hill, the sea is in the background, and she's trailing a gauzy scarf behind her, it billows in the wind, and it's almost as if she's covered her entire body in sequins because the way the white hot light is all around her, her body shimmers like a highway in the desert on a hot, hot day, and she is surrounded by a silvery halo. I can see that she is laughing and twirling and dancing and is completely unselfconscious and free. I've looked at my daughter all my life and I've never seen her quite this way before, but Angel Martinez has and he captured her and put her on this paper.

Late that night, I found the gallery's brochure in a tuxedo pocket.

RECENT PHOTOGRAPHS BY ANGEL MARTINEZ
ARIEL LIGHT AND DARK

I confiscated the photographs and demanded the negatives. These were given to me. Angel threw his camera into the Bay and smashed up his darkroom. Ariel disappeared that afternoon.

(SAMUEL *carries a white enamel basin of water.*)

She shaved herself. She did it alone. There are nicks and gashes on her, spots of blood, red bumps and chafing. Her hair is gone. She looks almost like everyone else now.

(HE *pours out the basin of water. It is full of blood.*)

AT SAID

BY GARY WINTER

A building superintendent, MR. CARLOS, *is trying to fix the pipes in Darra's apartment.* HE *answers her accusation that repairing pipes is more important to* HIM *than what she perceives as bigger world problems.*

SCENE
Darra's apartment, which is located in some isolated and impoverished American neighborhood

TIME
The present

MR. CARLOS: I don't think that way. You can but I don't. It's stupid, man. Being a building super is stupid. I know that and everyone knows that so what do you want me to do? You want me to go to Africa with a sandwich? Huh? You want I can kill that bus driver? I ain't no voodoo. I ain't sleeping heavy like that shit. I ain't remembering on the typewriter like Ms. Sybil. I don't have to. I got my pail and my hammer. I got my little girl. I had my wife, she became a whore so now she's sleeping in the gutter. I don't give a shit—I threw her out. You see that? I say fuck you whore we got things bad enough around here.

We got a daughter and you fucking with little shits in the stairwells? What they give you, witch? Bags of shit you can sniff on? Some stuff to shoot in you? That what you teach our girl? I say fuck you whore. I fucked her and I hear the bones crack, so what? What the fuck, some shit whore I marry, I was supposed to marry a princess?

I got a place. I fix the pipes. I take the garbage out. I got a daughter. So what, you fucking whore, you get straightened out if you want good things like I got. I work here so I got all this. So we got a daughter and she fucks it all up.

What—okay, gimme a plane ticket and I'll go to Africa and I'll give out sandwiches. You watch my girl and you fix the pipes. Take out the garbage. Clean the shit. Chase away the shooters in the stairwell. Push the bodies out of the way. Is that fair? I'll get souvenirs too.

What they got over there? They got pictures? They got postcards? They got dolls? They got dolls of the starving people? That anything you need, Ms. Darra? Make a list. Make a list.

[(*Darra puts paper in the typewriter and begins to type.*)

DARRA: For Mr. Carlos, to do: Feed the people. To buy: Doll. Rug. Toy. Beads. Postcards.]

AUNTIE MAYHEM
BY DAVID PUMO

CHARLOTTE, *a heavy-set man in his 30s, is a professional drag queen. Throughout his speech,* HE *sits at a table and removes his wig, shoes, jewelry, makeup, and other accessories.* HE *is speaking to Felony and Bobo, the occupants of the apartment, unconcerned that* HE *is interrupting them.*

SCENE
Somewhere in downtown Manhattan

TIME
Winter

CHARLOTTE: What a long night! What a fucking endless, miserable, tedious night. Marty missed three lighting cues. Every fucking sound cue is off. I almost stopped the show to strangle his fat, hairy neck. No tequila shots before the show, Marty. No fucking tequila shots — just say no! How many times I gotta tell him? You need to be sharp. You need to be quick. That's what coke is for. He's losing it. I'm gonna replace his ass by next week. This is not a fucking joke. This is art. This is my fucking reputation on that stage.

[(*By this point, Bobo is fed up with this interruption. He turns away from Felony and tries to go to sleep. Felony, having lost Bobo's attention, sits in bed and listens to* CHARLOTTE)]

CHARLOTTE: Then I spend two hours with Merle and Sandy. They really want me. They're doing a whole song and dance. They've got a bigger stage than Stingray, which they do. They've got state-of-the-art sound and lighting, which they don't, but it's better than the thirty-year-old shit I've been working with. They want a whole new show. They want to do a four-color ad. I've got complete creative control. . . . Do you know how much they offered me? Do you have any idea what they thought they could get away with? I just stared at them. What is this, a fucking workfare placement? I'm livid, but I manage to politely tell them what my going rate is. They start bargaining, like I'm a fucking flowerpot in Tijuana. I ordered one more gimlet, chugged it, and walked out. I'm not leaving Stingray to be treated worse somewhere else. I'm not climbing down the ladder of success. (HE *has taken off his wig, shoes, jewelry, makeup, etc.* HE *gets up to leave the room.*) I've had it. My feet are swollen. Please don't wake me up till at least Thursday.

THE BEGINNING OF AUGUST

BY TOM DONAGHY

JACKIE, *a new father in his early 30s, copes with the fact that his wife, Pam, abruptly left both* HIM *and their baby for no apparent reason. Here* JACKIE *tries to explain his side to Ben, who has asked* HIM *what* HE *did to make Pam leave.*

SCENE
The backyard of a nice suburban home

TIME
The present

JACKIE: What did I do? (*Beat.*) The thing I don't get is what *did* I do? You know? (*Beat.*) It's a two-way street. She's part of it. A few late nights! My friends over—and hardly ever. Hardly ever except Phil Miyale—who is a friend from college! Nothing was different. Nothing! (*Beat.*) She didn't like this one gift I wanted to give my Secret Santa. Inappropriate or something. This little ceramic thing. She's like, "It's not funny." Why did I even show her? She's like, "He won't get it." I knew the taste of my Secret Santa. Working on that account seven months and I don't know his taste? She's like, "People who have lupus don't like jokey gifts!" She's all the time here—she wasn't in my workforce, my environment. She had her own environment. Lupus isn't even always fatal! He's had it thirteen years! He didn't laugh at cheap jokes for thirteen years because of lupus? You learn to live with things. You better laugh or you just don't. She used to laugh at my jokes. Little teasing. Jokes at each other's expense. She'd laugh and laugh. Until she stopped. The minute she started working at that animal shelter the fun stopped. But then whenever I laughed with someone else, boy oh boy. Sitting there with that face. Stifling anyone else's enjoyment. Standing in the hallway with that face I hated. You just can't be silent with your face! That's why I got the new music system. Liven things up. Our songs! The ones we listened to! They're oldies now but they're good as new on that system! And she's all—she's fucking, "What do we need a new music system for?" Like I'm some ultraconsumer. Fuck you! I would never buy things. Never. And she's talking about buying? These catalogues? Her tastes were out of hand! Ordering things for the house from catalogues, state-of-the-art kitchen appliances—and who needed a garlic peeler? So your hands don't have to touch garlic! TOUCH SOME GARLIC FOR FUCK'S SAKE!

A BICYCLE COUNTRY

BY NILO CRUZ

In an effort to escape the poverty-stricken lifestyles they have in Cuba, Ines, Julio, and PEPE *depart their country on a raft, hoping to sail to Florida and begin a new life in the States. After several days at sea,* PEPE *has a vision, believing* HE *can walk on water.*

SCENE
On a raft in the middle of the Caribbean Sea. Projected on the Screen: Third Day Out at Sea.

TIME
The third day out at sea, probably in October/November 1993 (before the U.S. intervention on Cubans fleeing to the United States on rafts)

(JULIO *and* INES *are asleep.* PEPE *speaks to the sea.* HE*'s on top of the mast, looking out at the distance.* HE *is hallucinating.*)

PEPE: If your voice is coming from there, say something! (*Pause.*) If your voice is coming from there, say something! (*Pause.*) Push me! Push me, like you said you would. (*Sound of children laughing. A distant angelic aria. Then the continual sound of the rippling waves.*) Don't think you can play with my mind. You can't trick me. You're not going to make me lose my head. I'm not sentimental. I'm not. I'm like a fish. Scales. Sharp bones. You never see a fish cry. Why cry when fish live in the water. If I cry, I'll cry in the shower, enh! So no one can see my tears. Tears to the water. Water to the sea. (*Sound of roaring sea. The sound of a child calling someone in the distance. Then it all subsides.*) I've heard what the ocean does to people. I've heard. Like the desert. A fever. You see things. A mirage. You play tricks on the eyes. Whatever became of that day, eh? Whatever became of that day when I was a child, and my father brought the whole family together and said, "We're moving to the coast, and I'm going to show you the sea." And we sold all the chickens to buy the bus fare. We sold the cows and the pigs to rent a house close to the seashore. Look. . . . Look. . . . You can't trick me! I can close my eyes. . . . I can close my eyes and see you like that first day, when the driver said, "We're in Havana. We're by the seawall." And I climbed down from the bus, with my eyes closed, and my father said, "Open your eyes, Pepe. Open your eyes. This is the sea. This is the sea." And when I saw you, you were blue and big as the falling sky. Calm and full as bowl of blue soup. . . . You were all I imagined you to be.

Look. . . . Look. . . . Look at me running to you. (*Starts running in place.*) Look at me running to drink you! Look! Look! You can't trick me! (*Sound of children laughing.*) You can't trick me! You're not a lie! You're not a lie! You're not a lie! Look at me swimming! Look at me swimming! Look at me walking on your water, like Jesus. Julio! Ines! I'm walking on top of the sea like Jesus! (*Sound of a woman laughing in the distance. Julio and Ines wake up.*)

[JULIO: One can't even . . .]

(PEPE *continues running in place.*)

PEPE: I'm walking . . .

BIG BILL

BY A. R. GURNEY

WILLIAM TATEM TILDEN II, *otherwise known as* BIG BILL, *was one of the great sports stars of the twentieth century. Ranked number one in the world seven times,* HE *was instrumental in popularizing tennis in this country and, in 1920, was the first American ever to win Wimbledon.* TILDEN'*s life was dogged by his homosexuality, which surfaces unconsciously in the following speech.*

SCENE
The Germantown Cricket Club in Philadelphia

TIME
The twenties

TILDEN: (*To audience.*) Let's start with the golden rule of all athletics. Always play to win. Never play just not to lose. Every match is a battle, within and without. Cultivate a killer instinct in your soul, but be a sportsman to the world. Be murderous but courteous. The tough thing is to reconcile the two. (*Indicates his sweater.*) Which leads us to clothes. In tennis, we wear white. It's cooler, of course. And more attractive — by that I mean it's less likely to display unsightly patches of perspiration. And of course white makes the players more visible from the higher seats in the newer stadiums. And we always play better when we're watched, don't we? But there's yet another reason for whiteness. You'll notice that in the Bible the angels of the Lord always appear in white raiment. Why? Because white is pure, white is innocent. And tennis is an innocent game. That's why I don't approve of shorts. There's a young player in Grosse Point—good serve, exceptional net game—who wears shorts, at least in practice. I find it distracting. It says in the Bible, "Take no delight in a man's legs." Nor a woman's, either, I hasten to add. Men should wear long white trousers. Women, white stockings. The whiteness is what we want, not naked flesh. I hope we're all agreed on that. (*Taking up his racket.*) Now for the tool of our trade. Our Excalibur! (*Displays it.*) Consider the stringing. All rackets should be strung with gut, preferably taken from the intestines of a young lamb. . . . (*Strums his racket like a guitar.*) Listen to that sound. (*Sings.*) "Ain't she sweet. . . . Don't she knock you off your feet?" . . . Nowadays there is talk of shifting to manufactured fibers, but I much prefer real gut. It's organic, it has texture, it puts more spin on the ball. Keep it natural, say I. Natural strings in a wooden racket. Lately, in my wanderings, I've noticed that some players are beginning to wrap their grips with leather. They say their hands are less likely to slip. Not me. I like to sense the grain of the wood. It tells me where I am. (*Holds it up.*) My rod and my staff! It comforts me. (*Sits.*) Let's now talk about feet. (*Removes his shoes.*) Sneakers are important, of course. But not as important as shoe salesmen would have us believe. Many times during a match, I play in bare feet. (*Wiggles his toes.*) Why? Because you can feel the give of the grass. Or if it's clay, you can sense its density. You can dig in your heels or use your toes for purchase. (*Moves around.*) See? I'm grounded. I'm connected. . . . Ah, but I need a guinea pig. . . . (*Points off.*) You there.

[(*A young actor comes on hesitantly; call him Tony.*)

Tony: Me?]

TILDEN: Step out there, please. We'll demonstrate the basic stance in tennis.

[TONY: (*Proudly, grinning at audience.*) OK!]

TILDEN: (*Handing him the racket.*) Take the racket. That's it. Shake hands with it, as if it were the best friend you'll ever have—which it may turn out to be. (*Demonstrates.*) Good. Firmly, but not too tight. Give your fingers some play. Yes. Good. (*Stands behind him.*) Make sure that this V . . . this V for Victory . . . (*Reaching around, touching Tony's hand.*) between your thumb and forefinger, make sure it settles on the top of the handle. Yes. Now this is what we call the continental grip. (*The lesson becomes more intimate as* TILDEN *stands behind his pupil, with his hand on top of the pupil's hand, guiding his swing.*) Yes, all right now, stand sideways, like this, with your left leg forward. (*Moves Tony's leg forward.*) Yes. Now the ball is coming, so get your arm back in plenty of time, yes . . . good . . . now, now step forward and meet the ball out in front of you . . . there! Yes! And follow through all the way! (*They end in a strongly intimate position.*) There. That's your basic forehand drive. Build on that, and all will be well. (HE *steps away.*)

[(*Tony is obviously uncomfortable.*)]

TILDEN: Thank you, my young friend.

(*As Tony exits,* TILDEN *pats his rear with his racket, then begins to move gracefully around the stage, demonstrating the various strokes of tennis.*)

TILDEN: Because footwork is everything, people. You see? It's like a dance. . . . The serve . . . Pow!. . . the forehand . . . Pow! . . . the backhand . . . the rush to net . . . Pow, pow, pow! You see?

Look at me. I'm a dancer, really . . . I'm Nijinsky, I'm Valentino, I'm—who's that young dancer who performs on Broadway with his sister? I'm Fred Astaire! (HE *uses his racket as a cane.*) "Puttin' on the Ritz". . . . And I'm not being facetious here, folks. The player owes the gallery as much as the actor owes the audience. . . . (HE *calms down.*) But I've come to learn that the attention span of American audiences is somewhat limited, so that's enough lecture for tonight.

(HE *bows, salutes the audience with his racket.* HE *sits down and puts his shoes back on.*)

BIG LOVE
BY CHARLES MEE

This play is inspired by what some believe to be the earliest surviving play of the Western world, The Suppliant Women *by Aeschylus: Fifty young women flee their country to avoid marrying fifty male cousins. In the monologue, two of the would-be grooms have been discussing manhood, throwing themselves on the ground and hurling saw blades across the stage into a wood building.*

CONSTANTINE *stands panting, weeping.* HE *kicks the ground over and over — releasing the last spasms of rage, like little aftershocks, finally settling down.* HE *speaks very quietly.*

Or make of the monologue any character in any circumstance you like.

SCENE
A palatial home in Italy

TIME
Now

CONSTANTINE:
　　People think it's hard to be a woman;
　　but it's not easy

to be a man,
the expectations people have
that a man should be a civilized person
of course I think everyone should be civilized
men and women both
but when push comes to shove
say you have some bad people
who are invading your country
raping your own wives and daughters
and now we see:
this happens all the time
all around the world
and then a person wants a man
who can defend his home

you can say, yes, it was men who started this
there's no such thing as good guys and bad guys
only guys
and they kill people
but if you are a man who doesn't want to be a bad guy
and you try not to be a bad guy
it doesn't matter
because even if it is possible to be good
and you are good
when push comes to shove
and people need defending
then no one wants a good guy any more

then they want a man who can fuck someone up
who can go to his target like a bullet
burst all bonds
his blood hot
howling up the bank
rage in his heart

screaming
with every urge to vomit
the ground moving beneath his feet
the earth alive with pounding
the cry hammering in his heart
like tanked-up motors turned loose
with no brakes to hold them

this noxious world

and then when it's over
suddenly
when this impulse isn't called for any longer
a man is expected to put it away
carry on with life
as though he didn't have such impulses
or to know that, if he does,
he is a despicable person
and so it may be that when a man turns this violence on a
woman
in her bedroom
or in the midst of war
slamming her down, hitting her,
he should be esteemed for this
for informing her
about what it is that civilization really contains
the impulse to hurt side by side with the gentleness
the use of force as well as tenderness
the presence of coercion and necessity
because it has just been a luxury for her really
not to have to act on this impulse or even feel it
to let a man do it for her
so that she can stand aside and deplore it
whereas in reality

it is an inextricable part of the civilization in which she lives
on which she depends
that provides her a long life, longer usually than her husband,
and food and clothes
dining out in restaurants
and going on vacations to the oceanside
so that when a man turns it against her
he is showing her a different sort of civilized behavior really
that she should know and feel intimately
as he does
to know the truth of how it is to live on earth
to know this is part not just of him
but also of her life
not go through life denying it
pretending it belongs to another
rather knowing it as her own
feeling it as her own
feeling it as a part of life as intense as love
as lovely in its way as kindness
because to know this pain
is to know the whole of life
before we die
and not just some pretty piece of it
to know who we are
both of us together
this is a gift that a man can give a woman.

BITTER BIERCE
BY MAC WELLMAN

In the following speech from a play based on the life of American writer, journalist, and satirist AMBROSE BIERCE, *the title character recollects his newspaper coverage of a corrupt railroad tycoon, whose funding bill* HE *helped to defeat.*

SCENE
A public lecture hall

TIME
1897

BIERCE: Things livened up a bit in early 1896; Hearst wired me from New York: Railroad combination so strong in Washington that seems almost impossible to break them up, yet it is certainly the duty of all having interests of coast at heart to make the most strenuous efforts. Will you please go to Washington for the *Examiner?*

I replied.

I shall be glad to do whatever I can toward defeating Mr. Huntington's Funding Bill and shall start for Washington on Monday evening next.

Collis P. Huntington was the sole surviving appendage of the Bay Area Big Four — tycoons and swindlers — that had included Mark Hopkins, Charles Crocker, and Leland Stanford, by 1896 the latter three all mercifully dead.

The Southern Pacific and Union Pacific Railroads had been built using public monies loaned out at a reasonable rate of interest. The railroad men had enriched themselves enormously, at public expense, and had failed to make anything more than token repayment of either interest or principal (an amount conservatively estimated at seventy-five million dollars).

Mr. Huntington's Funding Bill was a ruse not merely intended to delay repayment for another thirty years, but in effect to assure that the issue of repayment would never be forced. The chief lobbyist for the corrupt and depraved railroad contingent in Congress was one John Boyd, whom I referred to as Huntington's tapeworm.

My first article began: Mr. Huntington is not altogether bad. Though severe, he is merciful. He tempers invective with falsehood. That is, although he says ugly things of the enemy, he has the tenderness to be careful that they are mainly lies.

Mr. Huntington appeared before the Committee and took his hands out of all pockets long enough to be sworn.

The spectacle of this old man standing on the brink of eternity, his pockets loaded with dishonest gold which he knows neither how to enjoy nor to whom to bequeath was one of the most pitiable it has been my lot to observe. He knows himself an outmate of every penal institution in the world; he deserves to hang from every branch of every tree of every state and territory penetrated by his railroads, with the sole exception of Nevada, which has no trees.

I called him an inflated old pigskin.

I called him a veteran calumniator.

I called him a promoted peasant.

I called him the swine of the century.

Of our modern forty thieves, Mr, Huntington is the surviving thirty-sixth.

One day I encountered Mr. Huntington on the steps of the Capitol.

Previously I had declined Huntington's hand in a committee session. It was once more offered. Met with stony rejection, Huntington finally shouted: Well, name your price; every man has a price.

My price is seventy-five million dollars, and you might make it payable to my good friend, the Secretary of the Treasury.

Later on someone asked the old reptile why he had approached me. Oh, I just wanted to see how big he was. And then added, now I know.

But that was the Mauve Decade. Once at the home of a Western family who had recently acquired a vast fortune, I was admonished by the hostess to notice her "spinal" staircase.

In January 1897 the Funding Bill was defeated and I returned to San Francisco.

THE BLACK MONK
BY DAVID RABE

ANDREI VASILICH KOVRIN—*an orphan, raised by a renowned horticulturalist—is a scholar and idealist in his 30s. The following monologue gives an early indication of his fragile mental state, which will deteriorate further during the course of the play.* HE *is speaking to Tanya, his future wife.*

SCENE
A flourishing Russian estate

TIME
Late 1800s

[TANYA: I think we should have sung something more lively and
    upbeat!]

KOVRIN: No, no, it wasn't the music.

[TANYA: The truth is, Kovrin, I find that serenade almost hypnotic.]

KOVRIN: No, no. It's something else entirely. I've been thinking all day
    of it, and growing more and more frustrated. It's this book—the
    one I was looking for. It contains a legend that I—

[TANYA: What legend?]

KOVRIN: I can't stop thinking about it.

[TANYA: Is it famous?]

KOVRIN: I'm fascinated by it and I feel the need to — but I can't find the book it's in. I've looked everywhere.

[TANYA: Could I have heard of it?]

KOVRIN: Of course, you could have [heard of it], but it's unlikely, because I have the feeling the source is esoteric. But it tells how one thousand years ago a monk, dressed in black, walked into the desert in Arabia. He walked over the sand, up and down the dunes, and in those very same minutes, fishermen hundreds of miles away saw a black monk gliding over the surface of a lake. [(*At the piano someone plays.*)] This second monk was a mirage. Now don't try to apply the laws of optics, because the legend pays no attention to them. Just listen to the rest. The mirage of the monk at the lake produced another identical mirage above it, and from that one came another, and on and on so that almost instantly, the mirage of the black monk was sent endlessly from one level of the atmosphere to the next, resulting in the Black Monk being seen in Africa and in Spain. There were Italians who saw him. People in the Far North. And all at the same time. And then he sailed right out of the earth's atmosphere into the heavens. (*This leaves* HIM *gazing up and out at the star-filled sky.*) And there he has roamed ever since, never finding the right conditions that might allow him to fade away. At the moment he might be seen on Mars, or near a star in the Southern Cross. (*Glancing at Tanya who gazes skyward.*) But the main point, the heart of the whole legend, is that exactly one thousand years from the day that monk first stepped into the desert, the mirage will come back to the earth. (*Once again* HE *studies the heavens as if expecting to see the Black Monk.*) . . . and people will see it. According to the legend, the thousand years is coming to an end. So we should be expecting the Black Monk any day now.

BLACK THANG

BY ATO ESSANDOH

Sam's best friend is JEROME, *a black man who says whatever* HE *wants, and* HE *has definite opinions on a number of subjects, including the fact that Sam is dating a white girl.*

SCENE
A bar. Sam and JEROME *are drinking beers.*

TIME
The present

JEROME: There is one thing that I have to warn you about, my brother. One very important thing that, as you embark on this new frontier of dating, you will find lacking. One thing that cannot be duplicated, cannot be replicated, cannot be approximated, or facsimilated. That one thing my brother . . . is the Ass. White women don't have It. They may think they have It. They may act like they have It. But they don't have It. They just don't. It's the law of nature. The amount of Ass, or the Ass Content per se, is directly proportional to the concentration of pigmentation in the skin. Therefore Sisters have high Ass Content while White girls and other pigmentally challenged females have low Ass Content. It's just the way it is. Can't do nothing about it. As a result, you will experience what I like to call A.W. . . . Ass Withdrawal. A.W. is a painful ordeal, my brother, and you may have thoughts of going back, but you must work it through because in the end, remember, it's for the best. Your case is particularly critical because you're going straight from sisters to white girls. See, I did me a couple of Puerto Ricans in order to ease the transition. You know what I'm saying?

BLACK THANG
BY ATO ESSANDOH

Sam has been sitting alone with a drink when JEROME *enters. There is an awkward pause as* JEROME *sits.*

SCENE
A bar

TIME
The present

JEROME: I knew this Indian chick once. You know, red dot on the forehead and all that shit. Her name was Sipi. Worked at the Foot Locker on Flatbush. She was something. Mad cute in the umpire stripes. Little black Converse on. The girl was fine, man. Fine ass little Sipi. Sold me a pair of Airwalks, the New Jordans when they came out. A pair of Reebok pumps. Remember Reebok pumps? The fly shit. Right? Sold me all kinds of shit. Socks, tees, my Knicks hat. Damn. I would just go in there sometimes, not even wanting to buy shit. Just check her out. She had this shy smile, the way she looked at me, all shy and shit. I think she was sweating me too. You know. So one time I'm like, "Yo check this out, I'ma roll up in there and ask for her number, and I'ma take her to Coney Island." You know, go slow because you could tell she was one of those slow girls. Take a whole six months before she'll let you even see her bra strap you know what I'm saying? Probably got to go to some funky ass holy temple and sacrifice a goat or some shit before she'll let you fuck her. You know what I mean? But she looked like she was worth it. You know them Indian people be some freaks behind closed doors. Kama Sutra? 'Nuff said. So I rolled up in there, had my pumps on, had my Knicks hat on with matching Reebok suit. Yeah, you know the deal. And I rolled up in there and I said, "A yo Sipi come here girl!" And she was all embarrassed and shit. Talking about, "Can I help you sir?" And I was like, "Yeah, you can help me . . . what's up with that red dot on your forehead girl somebody poke you or what?" You know, just trying to break the ice and shit. And she looked at me for a second . . . and started to cry. And I'm like, "Naw Sipi baby don't cry. I was just teasing. Shit I like the red dot!" And that was the truth. I was cool with the red dot. But she just kept crying like I stole her suede Pumas or something. So the manager, probably her father or some shit, comes out and says to me (*Mimicking Indian manager.*), "My friend. You must leave. You must leave right now my friend." And I'm like, "Yo can't I apologize? Can I say I'm sorry?" "No my friend you must leave. You must leave right now my friend. Or I call the cops." Shit what's this friend shit? You ain't my friend motherfucker! You ain't my friend! How you gonna call the cops on your friend? So anyway, they kicked me out. Banned me from Foot Locker. Imagine that? Ban a brother from Foot Locker? That shit ain't right. . . . I heard through the Foot Locker grapevine that Sipi went to med school a couple of years ago. I knew that girl was smart. Heard she got married too. Some Indian doctor. Two doctors in the house? They must be making bank! Wish I could see her again. Let her know I was cool with the red dot. . . .

THE BOSS'S DAUGHTER

BY JOSH MCILVAIN

MARTIN *is telling his friend (really the audience) about a recent amorous adventure with an old high-school chum and* MARTIN*'s boss's daughter.*

SCENE
The apartment of a friend

TIME
The present

MARTIN: Remember my old high school buddy Miles? Anyway, we keep in touch. Not the best of friends over the years but we keep in touch. He knows June, my boss's daughter, from college, and I'm not sure what their relationship was then but they've gone out for the past couple of years. He's a lawyer now for an entertainment firm. He's a rich kid. His father invented the dimmer switch. So Miles, June, and I get together in Hanesville where Miles lives and go to this cheesy suburban night club called Sergio's. Loud music, girls with lots of shit in their hair, expensive drinks. We're doing shots of Jagermeister which I haven't done since sophomore year in college but June likes it. Makes her crazy and as the night goes on, I keep feeling her foot rubbing against my leg. At first I think she's mistaking my leg for Miles's or maybe it's a joke but

I don't want to say anything because maybe it isn't. June goes off to the bathroom and Miles starts talking about how June's turned on by me and how he has this fantasy about watching her have sex with another man. So he makes this proposition . . . that if I'm willing, he'd like to watch me have sex with June. Well, I, what do you say to something like that? I said that's pretty crazy. He said not to worry, it's O.K. with him, he's into June exploring her sexual impulsiveness. I tell him I don't know I'll have to think about it. June comes back. We have some more drinks and I'm thinking this is wild, probably a real bad idea but honestly, it's been a while since I've had sex. My job gives me no time for a relationship. And June's got a real nice, firm body. So we leave. The plan was to go back to Miles's place and smoke some pot. But we start smoking in the car. I'm driving, June's in the passenger's seat and Miles is in the back. Well, I'm driving along, we're laughing, and she starts rubbing my leg and we're all joking about her rubbing my leg. For some reason it's hysterical. Then she works her way up and starts rubbing my crotch and I'm like "Whoa-ho-ho!" and Miles starts yelling, "Work it! Work it!" and she works it! Then she takes my hand and puts it between her legs. My hand goes up her skirt and she's got no underwear on. So I'm fingering her and I'm totally turned on but I'm also thinking, "This is nuts! This is nuts! I've got my hand in the boss's daughter!" Things get heavier, we start to quiet down and I hear this flapping sound from the back seat. I realize it's Miles jerking off. He starts yelling, "Pull over! Pull over!" So I turn off this road and go down to this boat ramp and park. June jumps on top of me. I still have my seat belt on and she's fucking me. Miles is laughing, hollering, and June's screaming. She's a screamer. But I'm looking at her face and it's dark and I can barely see it but what I do see looks just like her father so I say, "June! June! You've got to put a bag over your head!" She says, "Why?" and I say, "Because I work for your father and you look just like him and it's bothering the hell out of me!" Then Miles shoves a plastic bag forward from the back seat, saying, "Put it on! Put it on!" He's all into it. So she puts it on and we start fucking again and Miles is flapping away and June's got this plastic Rite-Aid bag over her head which she has me pulling down so it's tight on her face. Oh, it was sick. It was great too but it was sick, and I haven't hung out with them since. But anyway, I get to work on Monday and I see my boss and the first thing I see is the resemblance he has with his daughter, and from that day forward, I became a lot less afraid of him, and I'm doing a lot better at work now.

BURNING THE OLD MAN

BY KELLY MCALLISTER

Two brothers, Marty and BOBBY, *are on their way to the Burning Man Festival, an annual desert gathering based on radical self-expression, to bury their father's ashes.* BOBBY, *the younger, smokes weed in the back seat and sets their mother's car on fire. It then blows up.* BOBBY *is on the phone to his mother.*

SCENE
The lobby of a run-down motel

TIME
Summer

BOBBY: Hi, Mom. How's it going? I'm fine. Yeah, really. Totally fine. Well, we're still on the road. Listen, there was a little mishap with the car. Well, that's what I'm trying to tell you. We were driving along, me and Marty, and I was sitting in the back because Marty was going on and on about how evil women are for like the thousandth time, you know how he does, and I didn't feel like listening to that crap, so I got in the back and had a —well, I admit, I was smoking a cigarette—what? No, a regular cigarette. Well, he's lying. Mom, I don't smoke pot. Come on, what is this, high school? Honest, I was just smoking a regular old cancer stick.

I know. I will quit. I don't know. It's been a rough time. I know he had it. But that's not what he died of. I've been looking at his ashes for two days straight, contemplating cigarettes and bullets, and, you know, stuff. So, anyway, I was looking out the window at all that nothingness—you should see the desert. It's beautiful. Open land, huge skies like the ceiling in that cathedral in Germany, I think it's in Cologne—you know, that one I sent you the postcard from when I went there in high school—just awesome. I think I forgot how important it is to look at the sky, you know? Seems like all I do these days is forget things I shouldn't. So, I was looking at all this unspoiled beauty, and I got so wrapped up—I think I saw a coyote—that I forgot I had a burning cig in my hand, and it burnt down to my fingers and burnt me, and I dropped the cig out of reflex, and I swear to God it was out, but I guess it wasn't. And that's what happened. I'm really sorry. I didn't mean to burn your car up. I was just thinking about Dad, and how I'll never get to tell him about the desert, or anything, ever again, and I guess I got distracted. I know it's okay to be upset. Not too bad, more charred than burned, really. Oh, Marty's Marty, you know? I think he wants to go home, get his nose back to his grindstone, which is fine with me. Yeah, of course I'm still going. I don't know what he's going to do, and I don't care. You never know with him. I'm taking a cab from here. I don't know. Hold on. (*To Jo.*) How far is it to the Burning Man?

[**Jo:** That's just past Reno. About a hundred miles.]

Bobby: I see. (*Back to the phone.*) Kind of far. Yeah, I think I have enough. What, the Visa? Yeah, of course I still have it. I was keeping that for an emergency. Yeah, I guess it is. Okay. Thanks, Mom. Okay. I love you too. I won't. Ciao. (*Hangs up phone.*) Now, Miss, would you please call me a cab? One that takes credit cards?

CATCH & RELEASE

BY STACI SWEDEEN

In an effort to convince his new girlfriend to join him on a fishing trip, MICHAEL CECONI, *30, tells her the story about the first time* HE *went fishing with his father.* HE *possesses a seductive, bad-boy energy.*

SCENE
East Village, New York City

TIME
The present

MICHAEL: All right, so you never been out before, no big deal. You know what they say about your first time? You always remember it. My first time — I don't think I can do it justice. My old man — it was what he lived for. He was a real piece of work. He was what you'd call "craggy" — face full of scars, a cigarette hanging off his lower lip — but he loved to have a good time. I wish you could have met him. When I was growing up he'd talk about when he was a boy just learning the ropes and how he was gonna take me some day. I'd beg him to take me but he'd say no, he had his hands full with my older brothers. So off they'd go, leaving me home to raise holy hell with my mother. And when they got back, I'd make them go over every detail. He'd take me in the back yard to practice. I learned so much listening to him talk about how great a sport it is—but there are two things you gotta have. Technique and instinct. Amazing how much of life boils down to technique and instinct. And there are a lot of guys who think it should come easy, be a piece of cake, guys who've only seen the movies and think that all you got to do is dangle the bait. There are guys who never had anyone like my old man show them the right way, who don't understand about the skill involved, who insist on daylight when it's better in the dark. But hey, we all got to find our own way in life, right? That's what my dad always said. Michael, he said, you gotta project confidence. You gotta learn how to listen. You gotta be able to concentrate, figure out your position. Position is key. But also keep it simple, stupid. Don't get too concerned about the bumps and the groans in the night 'cause once you figure out your approach, your method, you're more than halfway home.

I was waiting for the day, man, I was waiting for the day.

The summer I turned 8, the old man decided I was finally old enough so he took me on this fishing trip that was unlike anything you've ever seen. See, at a certain time of year the salmon are swimming back up the river to spawn, and the state—the state would rather have you be able to take the fish out anyway, they're gonna die after they spawn, so you might as well take them out of the river and eat them. So at certain spots along the river, say in front of a dam or something, when the salmon have gone up as far as they can go—you'll have guys lined up practically shoulder to shoulder with this kind of snagging hook—a big three-pronged hook that's usually illegal—you have to use a different kind of line, too, not a lightweight sport fishing line but a heavyweight one in case you snag a rock you can pull it loose and not snap your line. So my dad and I went, it was getting dark and you have all these guys lined up, shoulder to shoulder, doing some of the most — aggressive fishing you've ever seen — throwing in, snagging, pulling out, throwing in — and hooks are flying everywhere, people just throwing and throwing. Sometimes a hook will land on someone — you know it when all of a sudden the guy next to you goes stiff — like this — cause if a hook hits you in the chest, say, if you hold still it'll most often just bounce off — or rip your shirt, but not catch the flesh. There are times, though, that — because everyone is just throwing and throwing — a hook will snag someone in the face, in the cheek, say — and if you move, or if the guy that snagged you pulls his line, you're hooked. And that's exactly what happened to my dad. He flinched — just a little — and then said to me, Michael, in my bag — get the clippers. I could see that the hook was through him, through his face and my heart started racing, but he kept real cool, real calm and said — bring those clippers over to me. So I did, my hand shaking. He pulled that fish hook out through his cheek, took that little clipper and clipped the end of the hook off. Then he told me to pull it through. And that's when I looked at his face and — got it. All those scars. And I looked around and saw all these guys surrounding us, guys who've been snagged — but they come back year after year. Like my dad. Like me. That's why I want to take you. You'll see. It's a great sport.

CHAUCER IN ROME
BY JOHN GUARE

In Rome to find his son and also on a pilgrimage for the millennium, RON *believes* HE *is confessing his sins to a priest and nun, impersonated by Matt and Sarah, friends of* RON'S *son, Pete. They are videotaping* RON *as part of an art project. All three are present for the confession.*

SCENE
The American Academy in Rome

TIME
July 2000

RON: That murder is like the facts of life. Would you teach sex to a kid? Kids learn sex on the streets. That's what the streets are for. To learn the brutal—if I may call them that—realities of life. Kids are cruel. I'm sure kids told him about the murder which happened the day the Pope came to New York back in 1965 to pray for peace. Lot of good that did. Pope Paul was the Pope then. That's thirty-five years ago. Does Pete know? Sure. He must know. But he never heard it from me. If he does remember it, he's forgotten it. I don't even remember it. It's the good part of being a kid. You forget. . . .

I visited my father in the prison farm where they put him. I brought Pete out. My father sat at the prison piano and played

"Deep in the Heart of Texas." "Rudolf the Red-Nosed Reindeer." The men who wrote those songs only wrote that one song and they lived like rajahs in the Taj Mahal forever. My father asked me who I was. "I'm your son." My father said, "You can't be my son. You're an old man. This is my son." And he kissed Pete over and over. This little boy—my son—Pete started crying. "Don't cry, boy. I'm writing you songs that'll make you rich." My father looked at me. "Are you an agent?" I said, "No, Dad, I'm not an agent." He turned away. "Thank you for coming." He kissed Pete, who he thought was me, over and over. "I'm going to write you one hit song that'll make you immortal and rich." And I pulled Pete away and we went back home to our apartment.

[RON *is quiet. Behind the screen, Sarah whispers to Pete.*

SARAH: Do you want me to stop him?

MATT: No.

PETE: No no—go on.]

RON: I look at that spot in the apartment where my father killed my mother. And I look at my wife who I hate and there is an undertow in Sunnyside and pretty soon I know I will do the same to her as my father did to my mother. Which is why I would like to have her sins forgiven before I do it because it's in my bloodstream—like me being an artist. My father wrote songs. I'm a painter—even if it's just signs. Pete—well, he'll be an artist. I know he's got it in him. It's in the genes. Like killing my wife. I need to know how my father felt. I know one day I'm going to put my feet in his footprints and do it.

Or maybe I'll write a hit song like "Rudolf the Red-Nosed Reindeer."

CHAUCER IN ROME

BY JOHN GUARE

As an artistic endeavor, PETE *urges friends Matt and Sarah to videotape his father's confession by pretending to be a priest and a nun. The confession is broadcast worldwide and results in* PETE'S *parents' murder/suicide.* HE *flees to an isolated island off of the coast of Sicily, has given up his profession as an art historian, and is a waiter in a restaurant, where the now-famous Matt and Sarah, who remain guilt-free, show up on their honeymoon.* PETE *refuses to acknowledge them, but does reflect on his own guilt over the episode.*

SCENE
A dive restaurant off the coast of Sicily

TIME
Summer 2001

PETE: When I was young — well, not so young — but young — school young — I loved my research. I loved being in the library, going off to museums, staring at paintings, wondering about the history behind each painting — not how it was made but where it fit into history — what had come before it and what came after. And I knew what I wanted to do with my life.

There was a young woman in my class who intrigued me because she also worked as a model for a life study class to support herself.

She was very funny and told me about the poses she had to strike during the day and how she loved being looked at while she was nude, *senza veli*—feeling all these pencils taking her shadow. She was not a very good scholar, but she was attractive beyond any experience I had ever had and she liked me—why? I don't know—perhaps she thought I could help her with a paper. The point is we met at the library one night and I walked her back to her apartment and she asked me in. Her one room was filled with charcoal drawings students had made of her body and then given her in token. I told her I did not have my pencil with me but would like to see what—to see how—well, we ended up in her pull-out—her bed. She lit candles. Her skin was even more luminescent than—do you know the paintings of De la Tour? Not important if you don't—

What terrified me that night about being with her was discovering the power here—in me—in my own body. The feeling she could generate in me. I did not feel that she gave it to me. She revealed to me what was in me—the joy, the ecstacy, the ecstatic state that was in me—that belonged to me, that I had read about but could not imagine that this potential for joy belonged to me—flowed in this body. We fucked and fucked and I finished and she said, "Will I see you tomorrow?" Did she say I love you? Yes. She slept and I got up and dressed and left her house quietly and ran and ran for many miles. The power that was in me—that I did not know was in me—that made my life so different—that changed my idea of who I was. I ran and ran.

I never called her again. I walked away if I saw her or else nodded and passed by. . . .

When I got the news that my parents had died because of an idea I had had—the power that was in me—I ran and ran and then ran further than I ever imagined and came here to this island off an island—and got a job.

CLEAN ALTERNATIVES
BY BRIAN DYKSTRA

Mr. Cutter *is a lawyer attempting to purchase the "pollution rights" from a small, struggling eco-friendly manufacturer. Here* He *relates his earlier quest for meaning with an exploration of Zen Buddhism. It didn't go well, so* He*'s off the spiritual path, probably for good.*

SCENE
An office

TIME
The present

Mr. Cutter: You're supposed to meditate on your question until you get past the Western Brain or the logic slave or the need to be right, and you simply have some kind of deep, spiritual answer. Probably not even in words. One by one the students are getting their questions and are silently led out of the room. I'm last. When we're alone, the Monk kneels next to me, his lips not an inch from my ear. On the tip of his tongue he has the question he wants me to consider for possibly forever. But he doesn't say it right away. I wait, my thoughts clear of things like impatience, excitement, anticipation. The question on his lips, the one I'm supposed to have on my mind, in my heart, take deep into my abdomen and consider from all angles of conscious, unconscious, and semiconscious thought, feeling, and awareness, the one that I hope will lead me into a place that will dissolve my suffering, my very own four-word Koan, leaves his lips: "Who Cut The Cheese?" . . . That's what he asked me. Who. Cut. The. Cheese. I suddenly find myself silently praying to Jesus (because some habits die hard) that he's kidding. But he smiles beatifically, and in case I hadn't heard that particular colloquialism, he asks, "You understand?" When I'm too crushed to answer he rephrases into the simpler, "Who farted?" And leaves me there. Alone. . . . Well, I can tell you I'll be god-damned if I'm going to squat in his cross-hairs for the next handful of years meditating on ass gas and who let one. The immediate answer that leapt to my brain was, "Who cut the cheese? Why, everybody, you orange-robe-wearing four-eyed Bucky-Beaver-looking half-Chink." What's he telling me? That he's looked into my soul, and what he's seen there is incompatible with this path I'm attempting to follow? That I'm too damaged to fix? Too much cocaine in the eighties? I don't think so, not with the way the old slut next to me looked. This fucking guy is having me on. Well, fuck that! I went out and did what I'd been wanting to do for the past two-and-a-half years and was too blissed out to realize. I went out, ate a hunk of sacred cow, killed half a fifth of some outrageously expensive single malt, re-hooked up with the Russian mistress, smoked a Cuban . . . and sued his ass.

I won, too. But the fuckin' Monk wouldn't play. He wouldn't cough it up. He defied the court, so I pressed and got him incarcerated for contempt. But he's a fuckin' Monk! Like he gives a shit where he has to spend twenty hours a day meditating. Prison is perfect for these people: shelter, food, and time! Then the bleeding-heart judge said they couldn't keep him indefinitely, so I settled for the next best thing and got his ass deported. Last I heard he got clipped in the latest purge in Tibet. Somebody pushed him through a sixteen-hundred-foot crevice in an ice wall on one of the Himalayan peaks, but fuck the guy. If he was as spiritual as he pretended to be, he should have sprouted wings and flown to brunch. He made his karmic water bed when he messed with me, so fine, he can freeze his nuts off in it, for all I care.

COMMUNICATING THROUGH THE SUNSET

BY KERRI KOCHANSKI

FRANKIE, 17, *the new kid in town, has been arguing with his dysfunctional friend, Rachel, a girl who has been sexually abused by her stepbrother.* FRANKIE *is secretly in love with Rachel, and in an effort to get closer to her,* HE *decides to reveal one of his deep, dark secrets.*

SCENE
A hill in the Midwest

TIME
The ethereal dusk

FRANKIE: There were these tadpoles. These tadpoles in my backyard. I'd sit for hours and watch as they'd swim in this pond where I'd built up my rock garden. I loved these things. . . . And it wasn't because they could swim fast. They couldn't. They were slow and wobbly. Morphing every day. Growing arms. One leg — they were ugly. Ugliest creatures I've ever seen!

Now spiders, maggots — I've seen them up close. Gross. Even for a guy. But the thing is, how did they get like — I mean, what was God thinking? To create organisms so completely —

(HE *takes a moment, as* HE *is completely blown away.*)

It's like the speed of light. Or black holes. Mind boggling. . . . But even more—because they're completely real. So thrilling to think—But how can we let ourselves? I mean, if we did. . . . Well, there would be no need to think of anything else. Watches would stop! Buildings would cease being built! So awed by their significance—

So we forget their importance. Forget their importance, in order to survive. To move along. Spend our lives in shallow actions prompted by shallow thoughts—

(*Coming to understand.*)

—which we *cling* to in order to cover up our awareness of what is most interesting—And why . . . ? Because that's what we as humans do. . . . We as humans don't think. We go along . . .

Miss Fitch. . . . You know, she tells us butterflies are beautiful, and so we pin them on the wall. . . . Well, I wouldn't pin a butterfly, any more than I'd pin a ladybug. Or a bee. I mean, what have they done. . . . Nothing like tadpoles. . . . Nothing like you, Rachel. Nothing like me.

(HE *turns to her.*)

You've got this ugly thing about you. . . . But just because there's something ugly . . . some scary thing like one arm or one leg—over which you have no control—because that's the way it was destined to grow because that's the way life took it— Well, just because you have that deformity, it doesn't mean you're not wanted . . . not by someone who can see that deformity for what it is. . . .

Tadpoles. . . . You know, I loved 'em so much I actually wanted to *be* one. . . . But aside from reincarnation, I knew I was never gonna get the chance. . . . So I did the next best thing. I ate 'em.

And it wasn't because I was freaky. And it wasn't because I was strange.

I just honestly love tadpoles.

CORPS VALUES
BY BRENDON BATES

A young Marine on leave for the funeral of his mother, CASEY TAYLOR *tells his retired Marine father that* HE *will not return to the base and that the burns* HE *received that earned* HIM *a medal were not from a car bomb.*

SCENE
The small rustic kitchen of the Taylors' nineteenth-century farmhouse

TIME
Late November 2004

CASEY: GO ON! You wanted to take a look, take a look. (HE *turns around. His back is covered with scars.*) These are not magnesium burns. There never was a car bomb. My C.O. claimed it to be so I wouldn't be . . . (*Chokes up.*)

[WADE: Huh?]

CASEY: I was having a smoke with my best friend, Badger. In Fallujah. We finally secured the area. The city was in ruin, quiet, motionless. We fought for three days straight. We hadn't slept in four. We were leaning up against a truck, happy to be alive. It was early morning and we just finished eating a can of peaches. He was telling me about his grandmother's Swedish pancakes and then, BANG, his skull exploded and my face was covered in his blood. I couldn't see anything for a few seconds. I heard two more shots. I heard my squad members taking cover. I quickly wiped the blood from my eyes and I saw this old woman charging at me, holding an AK-47. I don't know where she came from or how she got a hold of that rifle, but she looked like an angry grizzly bear dressed in rags. She pointed the rifle at me. I froze. She had the drop on me. I thought, *this is it*. And then I heard a few clicks. It was empty. So, I grabbed my rifle and charged at her. I cross-checked her to the ground. Knocked the wind out of her. I grabbed her weapon and threw it behind me. I pointed my rifle at her and told her not to move. Then I heard someone say, *Badger is dead*. And something came over me — I don't know what. I didn't care who this woman was; she killed Badger — my best friend, my *brother*. So, I walked over to the truck while she laid on the ground, gasping for air. I grabbed a five-gallon jerry-can out of the back, opened it, walked back over to her, and dumped the whole thing on her head, covering her in gas. Everyone watched me do it. I told Private Brady to hand me his book of matches. He did. Without hesitation. I took it from him, opened it, struck a match, and threw it on her. She went up so quick. Like a brush fire in a high wind. She let out this *scream* that pierced my ears; it shook my whole body. That scream . . . it was the same scream I heard when I killed that young boy. It was his mother. Her scream awoke something inside of me and, all of a sudden, I was seeing this 50-year-old woman burning alive right in front of me, rolling around on the ground. And I realized what I had done. And I wanted to save her. I wanted to ease her pain. I should've just shot her, put her out of her misery, but — for some reason — I thought I could put out the flames and save her. So I hurled myself onto her, hoping to smother the flames. That's when I caught on fire. My men saved me before any serious damage was done, but not before the flames left their mark.

(*Pause.* [*Wade looks at the burns.*])

CASEY: Don't look at me like you've never seen shit like this before. You've seen it. You lived through Vietnam — *Vietnam* — and you still let this *stupid fucking war happen . . . again*! Why didn't you take a *stand*? How could you just *let it happen*? Did you learn nothing? What does it take to get this fucking world to do what is right?!?!? We just keep passing down our sins. From one generation to the next. (*Points to himself.*) Well, it stops *here*! I will not pass these scars down to my son. I don't care WHAT IT TAKES! I will bear these burns all the way to my fucking grave and they will decay into the fucking dirt . . . (*Grabs his shirt off the floor.* HE *struggles to slide it over his burns.*)

CUBAN OPERATOR, PLEASE
BY ADRIÁN RODRÍGUEZ

ABEL, *a young Cuban-American of about 30, is anticipating the death of his father.* HE *holds a picture of his father as a young man in a baseball uniform.*

SCENE
A modest apartment in Union City, New Jersey

TIME
2000

ABEL: (*Very peacefully.*) This is my favorite picture of my father. It's a picture of him in a baseball uniform with some of his teammates. Only one thing made him look like the man that was so far away. Baseball. (*Pause.*) He loved baseball.

[*Father walks over to sofa and looks at picture held by* ABEL *and smiles.* HE *continues looking at the picture for a few seconds while* ABEL *speaks and then he returns to his rocking chair.*]

ABEL: The man in the picture, the man my father used to be before having to abandon everything, was known as "El Americano," the American. He must be 16 years old in this picture. Starting pitcher of the Estrellas de Collante, a semi-professional team financed by the private hospital at Collante. The man in this picture was a semi-professional baseball player. He looks proud, smug, cocky, confident. He once told me that his team had traveled to a local town named Fomento for a game. He was going to pitch since it was an important game and he was the best pitcher on the squad. Before the game they were invited to have breakfast at a local restaurant and as he was eating he noticed a group of young women asking one of his teammates who El Americano was. They wanted to see the famous pitcher who overpowered his opponents with speed. When he was pointed out, one of the young women remarked, surprised: *¿Aquél flaco es el Americano?* That skinny guy over there is the "American"? Utter disbelief. That 105-pound 16-year-old boy with enormous ears was expected to go to the majors to play with the Americans? Yes he was, and he pitched a shutout game that afternoon to prove it. He would soon be in Havana playing with the Americans. I could see it in his eyes.

DEDICATION OR THE STUFF OF DREAMS
BY TERRENCE MCNALLY

An actor producing children's plays in a cramped space in a strip mall, Louis Nuncle *dreams of owning his own theatre. As a birthday "surprise," his partner, Jessie, finagles* Him *a special visit to a beautiful old neglected theatre building in their upstate New York town.* Lou *fantasizes about bringing this decayed room to life.*

SCENE
The stage of an old theatre

TIME
Now

Lou: So, here I am, center stage, solus, on a real stage in a real theatre. A stage and theatre that by rights should belong to me and not some alcoholic millionaire who is letting it go beyond all repair or reason. By what rights is it mine? Divine rights, artistic rights, moral ones. Not that they count for much in these impoverished times when wealth equals good and big equals better. I would transform this shabby, forgotten, forlorn room into a place of wonder and imagination again. That chandelier would sparkle anew if I had to polish every crystal myself. The aisles would be newly carpeted in a gesture of welcome and respect. Those rows of broken seats would be reclaimed in a plush red velvet that said,

"Sit down, children, you are safe here. We are going to take you on a wonderful journey to China or Persia or Timbuktu." Today we are going to tell you the amazing story of your favorite character, anyone you choose. But before we begin, there are a few rules, so listen up. I said listen up, you kids in the balcony. That means you, too. No kicking the seat in front of you. No paper airplanes or spitballs. No putting chewing gum under the arms or seat of your chair. No talking, unless the action becomes so unbearably exciting that you have to call out: "Turn around, Robin Hood, quick, the Sheriff is going to kill you." Or so sad that you won't be able to live if you don't speak up. It's up to you that Tinker Bell doesn't die, that Abraham doesn't sacrifice his firstborn. For the precious time that you are here and we actors are before you, the future of the world is in your hands, the fate of the human race is yours to decide. Think about it. The possibilities are boundless, the responsibility is yours. And don't forget to breathe! I know, we all forget to sometimes in the theatre. Me, too. I also stop breathing, it's so wonderful. (HE *takes in a deep breath, then lets it out.*) And always the curtain will fall, the story will have ended, and we actors will take our bows. Houselights up! It's over. We can all go home now. But something has changed. Tinker Bell has lived. Cinderella has found her Prince. You will go back to your real world and it will still be raw and painful, ugly even, but maybe a little less so because of what you have seen here today. Harmony and happiness *were* possible. And I will go back to my real world and it, too, will be a little more bearable, a little less unbearable because of what I have given you—and in giving you, have given myself: love and laughter, which are a good deal more nourishing at your age than bread and games. Hell, at *any* age. You lucky, lucky children. When I was your age, I didn't have a theatre in my life. I had to invent one of my own. All I had was a mirror, my mother's closet, and my music.

(*Strains of Tchaikovsky's* Sleeping Beauty.)

I'm telling you a secret now. A secret no one knows but you — not even Jessie, and I tell her everything. Well, almost everything. I would go to my mother's closet and take out her fullest skirt. I would put on the music I loved the best, the *Sleeping Beauty* — it was a waltz — and start to twirl in front of the mirror. Slow, slow I'd twirl, in-a-trance kind of slow. For hours sometimes. It felt like forever.

THE DOG PROBLEM

BY DAVID RABE

RONNIE, *20s, one of the neighborhood guys, divulges a secret.*

SCENE
A lamppost near a dumpster in Lower Manhattan

TIME
Today

RONNIE: Anyway, what the fuck—you should know that I have Psychic Powers.

[JOEY: Who? You?

(JOEY *is laughing.*)]

RONNIE: Yeah.

[JOEY: But you're a joke.

RONNIE: Well, maybe.] It's not something I can count on, or you know, just summon up on demand. [(JOEY, *amused and dismissive, shakes his head and starts away.*)] Because they just come over me, these psychic powers, like in a wave, all these thoughts about people and what they done. Like you — (*This stops* JOEY.) — you were married twice before, weren't you.

[JOEY: No.]

RONNIE: How many times you been married? (*Wait.*)

[JOEY: (*Returning, annoyed.*) I never been married.]

RONNIE: You never been married?

[JOEY: No.]

RONNIE: Never?

[JOEY: I had some girlfriends.

RONNIE: No, no it's more than girlfriends.] What am I doin' here? I'm messin' it up. Maybe I'm thinking too much, maybe I'm showing off. Because what I'm getting off you is about this woman, and she's in love with you!

[JOEY: What woman?]

RONNIE: And I'm getting this old apartment building on the corner and you are a kid on the fire escape — you're climbing up and you're going one two three four five six — (*Stopping, realizing.*) You're a kid! A kid! So of course you couldn't be married. But it's that kind of love — that's what mixed me up, because if you coulda married this woman, you woulda. But you're a kid, see, and it's six — no, five stories to this window with white curtains on it, white curtains with apples pictured on faded cloth, faded apples, faded curtains and leaves — it's all fucking faded. [(*Facing* JOEY.)] Where is this? What am I seeing?

[**JOEY:** Keep going!]

RONNIE: There's a woman inside and you want to go see her, you want to go visit her, but you're afraid. I don't know why you're afraid. It's because of something—I mean somebody else, not her, but her husband. Except he isn't really her husband. I mean, you didn't know that then, but you do now—he was just this man, who was in her house all the time and he hated you, but he isn't home. You could have come up the front way and knocked, but you're trying to see in to find out if he's there, and you make a noise and you hide. You're ashamed of sneaking and afraid of the man and you don't want anybody to see you, so you back up into the shadows. And she sticks her head out, but she doesn't see you. Her hair is red, it's all tangled, all tangled. Long. Falling down around her shoulders. She's got something in her hand, it's a—rosary—white with big beads, and she drops it as she looks out, and she reaches, and loses her balance, reaching for the rosary, spinning through the air, and she follows it. She grabs at the air and turns in the air, and she sees you. She sees you and your eyes meet and she says your name—she says, "Joey," and she sees you standing there watching— (*His fingers fall from the lamppost like a tiny figure falling.*) as she drops down into the dark of the alley below. Who was that, Joey? (*As* JOEY *turns, moves away toward the dumpster.*) Do you know who that was?

DOUBT

BY JOHN PATRICK SHANLEY

FATHER FLYNN, *a priest who will soon be accused of molesting a male student, gives a group of young men some tips on basketball as well as personal hygiene. The lights crossfade to* FATHER FLYNN, *whistle around his neck, in a sweatshirt and pants, holding a basketball.*

SCENE
School playground

TIME
The present

FLYNN: All right, settle down, boys. Now the thing about shooting from the foul line: It's psychological. The rest of the game you're cooperating with your teammates, you're competing against the other team. But at the foul line, it's you against yourself. And the danger is: You start to think. When you think, you stop breathing. Your body locks up. So you have to remember to relax. Take a breath, unlock your knees—this is something for you to watch, Jimmy. You stand like a parking meter. Come up with a routine of what you do. Shift your weight, move your hips. . . . You think that's funny, Ralph? What's funny is you never getting a foul shot. Don't worry if you look silly. They won't think you're silly if you get the basket. Come up with a routine, concentrate on the routine, and you'll forget to get tensed up. Now on another matter, I've noticed several of you guys have dirty nails. I don't want to see that. I'm not talking about the length of your nails, I'm talking about cleanliness. See? Look at my nails. They're long, I like them a little long, but look at how clean they are. That makes it okay. There was a kid I grew up with, Timmy Mathisson, never had clean nails, and he'd stick his fingers up his nose, in his mouth— This is a true story, learn to listen! He got spinal meningitis and died a horrible death. Sometimes it's the little things that get you. You try to talk to a girl with those filthy paws, Mr. Conroy, she's gonna take off like she's being chased by the Red Chinese! (*Reacting genially to laughter.*) All right, all right. You guys, what am I gonna do with you? Get dressed, come on over to the rectory, have some Kool-Aid and cookies, we'll have a bull session. (*Blows his whistle.*) Go!

DUST
BY CARRIE LOUISE NUTT

THE CLEANER *is not only the killer Frankie has hired to eliminate her former husband, but later* HE *turns out to be* MIKE, *a childhood friend of Frankie's present boyfriend.* THE CLEANER *is now out of prison and trying to start a new life as a preacher.* HE *has broken into Frankie's apartment and is holding a gun on her and her former husband.*

SCENE
Eastern Washington

TIME
The present

THE CLEANER: It's people like you that make living in this world a miserable experience because we have no protection. It's the minions of Satan. The spawn, shall we say: the abortionists, the child molesters, the drug users, the homosexuals and the idolaters. They have forced God to remove His protection from us, making this great place—as they say—Hell on earth. But let's remember this is God's country! Paradise! We have His ear. We are His people. He has given us wealth and power and we *can* get right with Him! We *can* win back His protection. We have to put God back in the house, the schools, the government. We have to win the war on immorality!

God has handed me, like Michael, a swift sword to wreak His vengeance upon any foe who dares to undermine His plan for us. To strike down those who have led us astray, to clean up and reassert that which is good and right and Godly in this country. I have been sent by God, into the bed of sin to protect Eden, and I am not about to see the Feminazis and prostitutes, the Teletubbies and the black people make us subjects to Evil by angering the good Lord with their worldly, and otherwise negligently secular ways. I will not be proverbially—or literally—banished from Paradise. Because I know what that is like, and I refuse to go back. To backslide.

This is Paradise. Here. On earth. Aside from all the greedy iconographers, the prideful sinners and the oversexed homosexuals, who would like to promote their agenda, and ultimately, seize power. They are working to convert our children, youth targeting. Targeting the innocent. Just like the tobacco industry. I mean, obviously, Satan is at work here.

You should really come to a meeting, Ms. Simmons. I think you'd find it—of course, I'm not sure women are allowed, especially your type. Are you a Feminist? Because Feminists have long escaped the wrath of God's angels without mercy, but believe me, you Feminazis are responsible for the deterioration of the family, as are lesbians and abortionists, but PEE is a well-regarded organization, and if you meet the requirements, you might be interested in looking into us. We're working on spreading the Word. And soon, PEE will be recognized as a purveyor of the Good, and also as a grass-roots success, which is an important part of the movement for reclamation of culture and morality.

Secretly, and this is just between us three, well, four, we're hoping the good Lord will see our work and send us one of his evangelicals to preside over a meeting, but we know we have a long spiritual mountain to climb before we get there.

Okay, now, if you don't mind, Ms. Simmons, the Lord wants you to sit down. Sit your ass down.

DUST

BY CARRIE LOUISE NUTT

Speaking to Bo, his ex-wife's lover, EVAN *recalls his chaotic relationship with his ex, Frankie, which started in grade school.*

SCENE
Eastern Washington

TIME
The present

EVAN: Me and Frankie, we've known each other since we were little kids. Probably 6, 7. Something like that. We were in grade school. I stepped on her heels cause I . . . I thought she was cute. She punched me, broke my nose. I bled all over. My pants, my shirt, the floor. That was how we met. She has a way of making you hold on when you know it's gonna kill you. One time, years ago, this was before . . . *before.*

Anyway, we decided to get drunk and go swimming. So we drove down the valley, winding our way between the long grass and pine trees, 'til we hit this bend, where the river widens. Every summer, this is where people go. It's called Driller's Pool. We parked the car. Rolled the windows down. Lit up. Drank beer after beer, just talking. Not hating each other. She had her feet up on the dash.

Leaving footprints on the window, even though I told her not to. She always did what she did cause she wanted. Didn't matter what you said. There was so much then, you know. Life was good and it was simple. It was enough just to be barefoot in the dirt with a Bud. Anyway, we got nice and toasty, made our way to the water and were standing on the last couple of steps, when I said something about her ass. Something mean-spirited, probably. I don't know. I laughed. She didn't say nothing. We climbed into the water, and before I knew it, she was on top of me, pressing my head under. Holding me like that. And I was drowning. Got a mouthful of water in my lungs. Couldn't breathe. I was hitting her and pulling, but she wouldn't let go. I nearly passed out 'fore she let me up. And still she didn't say nothing. Just climbed out. Walked back to the car. Stripped, wrapped herself in a towel and finished the case.

END ZONE

BY BOB SHUMAN

While HE *mixes drinks and unwraps takeout food,* ARTHUR
TRAINER — *a freelance composer and percussionist (late 30s) — talks
to his father (late 70s).* THEY *haven't seen each other in seven years.*

SCENE
*A motel. It's about a mile down the road from a prep school in the
Northeast. Two adjoining rooms have been rented.*

TIME
Several years ago, in November

ARTHUR: You go ahead and eat if you can't wait. I thought you'd like
Old Fitzgerald and lemon, Dad, like sitting out in your garden. You
and Norm during the summer, building, digging — boxwood: a
Jeffersonian ideal. Seven years old. Running away. You remember
me? Down by the lake to the powerhouse — (*About his drink.*)
Should make this a little stronger. The man who painted in the
boiler room. Always in the dark, waiting for his pictures to dry.
Dwight. Painting without models; used dirty magazines instead.
(*Pause.*)

Carting sand and bricks in the wheelbarrow. Ivy, mountain
laurel, replica Greek statuary, the Brussels "Statue of Piss!" (*Pause.*

Continuing to make drink.) I don't care what anybody thinks of me, Dad—mi' as well teach like you wanted. Been fired four times, I keep telling people the truth! (*About the drink.*) What's the matter? This is your favorite. Old Fitzgerald and lemonade. (*Pause.*)

I'm supposed to watch you two from the magnolia tree. Rhododendron being planted. Pretend I'm sweeping leaves. "Don't come over here, stay over there, get out of the way!" No more powerhouse trips, no more rafting, no more hikes across the bridge. Drifting farther off on the hot grass, and . . . walk right into town, just like that, past bullies and vagrants, Mr. Jackson delivering groceries, end up petting the Dalmatian in the firehouse. (*About the drink.*) This is too sweet, they don't make that kind of lemonade, looked all over for it. Shoulda gotten mint. (*Pause.*)

I was so afraid you were going to die, Dad. I don't know why. There wasn't anything wrong with you, I just found out people . . . die. Mom in India studying the Taj Mahal. Norm says when that number comes up you're on your own.

Out to the overpass to break bottles. Balancing on planks at the lumber yard. We were playing hide and seek, Dad. Flatten coins on the tracks, pumping my arm up and down for the conductors to blow the whistle. Over to the woods where that boy and girl from the high school committed suicide. . . . Rumors among the faculty, Dwight molested a kid. (*Pause.*)

(*In his father's voice.*) "Don't know what's the matter with you, become a nuisance!" You grab my hand tight. Sometimes picking me up, walking so fast, "get you home." Past cookouts and 4-H clubs, ghosts in the graveyard. Back to the construction of my maximum security pen—destined to become the place where

I'd be dumped after school while teams made championships and Mother's anthropology clubs won prizes. To think that your continually growing creation of intricately designed brickwork with window boxes, slate landings, mini-turrets, a sundial, and birdbath—even an ice-skating area, as well as white picket fencing—should have been built to rein in one lousy pain-in-the ass kid! (*Pause.*) It really wasn't though, was it? It wasn't for Mom—and it wasn't even for sitting outside and having bourbon and lemonade. It was something to do during a summer; demonstrating the deep bonding between a father and son: you and Norm. (*Pause.*) Come on, let's get you set up! One drink isn't going to hurt you. This is a celebration. Clayt offered me a job, back here for the spring. They think I know something about music even. (*Silence.*)

I want to visit Dwight. Purples, dark canvases, umbers. My days are numbered, the new yard almost complete. . . . (*Pause.*) I know the route where I won't get caught—find a feather, blow a dandelion's top off. Past the Quonset huts, across the campus gravel walks. (*Suddenly, loud.*) "HEY! YOU GET OUT OF THERE!" (*As if seeing him.*) Norm. Both of us stop. (*Pause.*) He knows where I'm headed. Chasing me, blood pulsing through my neck. "DOWN BY THE LAKE!" Running me down, shoving me, on top. Pulling, won't let me go, I'm falling, pushing me. It's you! Heard him. Hold my hand, dragging me, find rope, I'm biting. Against the magnolia. "Put him up there." Norm telling me to "eat that bark."

No wonder somebody called the cops! Tying, pulling it tighter! No wonder they called! "Won't run away again!" Vomit across the sidewalk. I can't breathe . . . like now! I'm glad somebody called. . . . I'm glad they saw it. (*Pause.*) I wanted you to die.

(ARTHUR *throws the glass, shattering it.*)

THE EXONERATED

BY JESSICA BLANK AND ERIK JENSEN

In this play, six former death-row inmates, now exonerated, tell their stories. KERRY *is a 19-year-old, trapped in a 45-year-old's body. Born and bred in Texas, and with a strong Texas accent,* KERRY *is a white male, wrongly imprisoned for twenty-two of his forty-five years, and eager to rediscover the world.*

SCENE
Minimal set pieces, perhaps a straight chair

TIME
The present

KERRY: It actually started when I was in the ninth or tenth grade: Me and my friends would, you know, act like we were going to school and then run out the back door and start trying to find a car with the keys in it. And I had the misfortune that one of the cars that I stole, in my adventures to conquer the world, was the sheriff deputy's car and I, ah . . . wrecked it—driver's ed I didn't take—and, make a long story short, the deputy beat me for it.

And that was pretty much it — after that, any robbery, any broken window, any cat up a tree, everything was just *my fault*, as far as the sheriff was concerned.

And then, fast-forwarding, I'm 19 and I'm at this apartment complex in Texas, called the Embarcadero — there's a swimming pool there; it's where all the hip people hang out. And I was an attractive guy; I dressed real nice. It was the seventies, you know, man, I bought my clothes from the hippest place, like the Gap, and I had my hair styled real long, platform shoes and bell-bottoms. I looked tight. And I was walkin' towards the swimming pool, and there was this beautiful gorgeous girl, man.

[(*To* SANDRA.) Not as pretty as you.

SANDRA: Go on.]

KERRY: But really *gorgeous*, man — just nude and fondling herself, right there in the window. So I look up and I go, "Oh my God, man . . . wow." 'Cause I had lived a very sheltered, naïve life, I'd never even been to a strip club before — and I'm seeing this total complete mature woman, and I'm goin', "Okay, yeah, that's cool, man."

And so anyway, a couple days go by, and I'm back at the pool and there's this chick layin' out there. To make a long story short, we started talking, told her I was a bartender in Dallas — course I was working at a gay bar, but I didn't tell her that — I'm just stretching everything as much as I can because I want to be all that plus a bag of potater chips. Anyway, we end up going back to her apartment. . . . We . . . uh . . . you know . . . made out.

[**SANDRA:** (*To audience.*) But not . . . all the way.

KERRY: Oh, no, no, no.] I was in there for about maybe thirty, forty-five minutes, whatever, and I got cold feet because she was so aggressive, and I left.

And I didn't ever see or hear from her ever again until I'm arrested for her murder three months later, August of 1977.

EXPECTING ISABEL
BY LISA LOOMER

NICK *and Miranda have been trying to conceive a baby—by every means known to science—but without success. Their efforts have put a strain on their marriage which results in a fight and a breakup.* NICK *is alone on stage.*

SCENE
An empty stage

TIME
The present

NICK: (*To audience.*) Okay, I'm gonna pick up the story and help her out. But first, you gotta understand something. I don't like to yell at my wife in the middle of Columbus Avenue—who does that? I was taught to turn the other cheek! Besides, you talked back, some nun'd pull your sideburns. And let me tell you something else. Until I met that hamster—I was a pretty happy guy! (*Glances offstage.*) Unlike some people. . . . Sure I saw some bad things go down when I was a kid—who didn't? I saw Nino Gallata push his brother off a balcony when they were moving furniture. Palmer Di Fonzo—I cut off his eyebrow accidentally with a pen knife—his mother came after me with a gun. Hercules Sorgini, smallest kid on the block, broke his neck in a sled accident, it was like this— (*Leans head on right shoulder.*) For a year they called him "Ten After Six." And Wee Wee Scomo had a heart attack right on the dance floor in junior high. Doing the Twist. He jumped up, did some splits, never got up again. Best dancer at Holy Savior. What are you gonna do? You gonna tell a kid, "Wee Wee—don't dance"? Besides— (*Glances offstage.*) If his mother had worried about violent television and the crap they put in the school lunches—would it have saved him from the Twist!? (*Yells offstage.*) THAT'S WHY I DON'T WORRY! (*To audience.*) And that's why I've always been a happy guy. Like when I go to the bank. I don't think, "Oh shit— (*À la Miranda.*) "What if the guy on the other side of the cash machine's got a drug problem?" I don't even cup my hand over the keypad when I punch in my pin, which happens to be "Jude," by the way, after the patron saint of lost causes—and not on my worst days—not even on the day my wife left me on Columbus Avenue would I have had a problem telling you that—'cause, hey, if you wanted to go out later, and use my favorite saint's name to steal my money— (*Yells offstage.*) I JUST WASN'T GONNA WORRY ABOUT IT! Besides . . . (*Pause; remembers.*) I didn't have any money. I spent my last fifty bucks on paint for the baby's room. And then we sold the apartment. Pretty fast, too, because the couple who bought it were expecting a baby any day. Then me and Miranda had that fight in front of this Starbucks they put up where my favorite used art-book store used to be. . . . Then she went down to the sperm bank. . . . (*Distraught.*) I did what any guy'd do— (*Pause.*) I went home to my mother. [*His mother enters and kisses* HIM *on both cheeks.*]

FABULATION, OR THE RE-EDUCATION OF UNDINE

BY LYNN NOTTAGE

At a gathering of recovering drug addicts, ADDICT #1 *recounts his descent from a popular and highly respected college English professor to a common criminal due to his crack cocaine habit.*

SCENE
New York City

TIME
The present

ADDICT #1: I miss it. I miss the taste and the smell of cocaine, that indescribable surge of confidence that fills the lungs. The numbness at the tip of my tongue, that sour metallic taste of really good blow. (*The addicts savor the moment. "Mmm."*) It was perfect, I mean in the middle of the day I'd excuse myself and slip out of an important faculty meeting, go to the stairwell and suck in fifteen, twenty, thirty dollars worth of crack. (ADDICT #1 *pretends to inhale. "Mmm."*) I'd return a few minutes later full of energy, ideas, inspired, and then go teach a course on early American literature and not give a God damn. In fact the students admired my bold, gutsy, devil-may-care attitude. Why? Because I'd lecture brilliantly and passionately on books . . . I hadn't read. Indeed, the university didn't know how high and mighty I was when they promoted me chair of the English department and gave me an office with a view of Jersey. It was fantastic, I could smoke crack all day, every day in my office, seated in my leather chair, at my solid oak desk. It was near perfect, it was as close to nirvana as a junkie can achieve. But my colleagues were always on my case. "Beep, Mr. Logan wants you to attend a panel on the symbolism of the tomahawk in *The Deerslayer*. Beep, Beep, Ms. Cortini is here for her thesis defense, what should I tell her?" Those thesis-writing motherfuckers drove me crazy. And I wanted to kill them. But you know what happens. I don't have to tell any of you junkies. "Beep, President Sayer wants to see you in his office. Right this minute. Beep. He's getting impatient." Fuck you! But by that time I was on a four-day binge, my corduroy blazer stank like Chinatown. And I was paraded through the hallowed halls like some pathetic cocaine poster child. But I don't remember when I became a criminal, but it happened at some point after that. The descent was classic, it's not even worthy of detail. Blah, blah, blah.

FAT PIG
BY NEIL LABUTE

A somewhat narcissistic, shallow 20-something, CARTER *tries to apologize to his friend Tom after making fun of his overweight girlfriend by talking about his own reaction to his "fat" mother.*

SCENE
A big city near the ocean

TIME
The present

CARTER: I used to walk ahead of her in the mall, or, you know, not tell her about stuff at school so there wouldn't be, whatever. My own *mom*. I mean . . . I'm 15 and worried about every little thing, and I've got this fucking *sumo wrestler* in a housecoat trailing around behind me. That's about as bad as it can get! I'm not kidding you. And the thing was, I blamed her for it. I mean, it wasn't a disease or like some people have, thyroid or that type of deal . . . she just shoveled shit into her mouth all the time, had a few kids, and, bang, she's up there at 350, maybe more. It used to seriously piss me off. My dad was always working late . . . golfing on weekends, and I knew it was because of her. It had to be! How's he gonna love something that looks like that, get all sexy with her? I'm just a kid at the time, but I can remember thinking that.

[Tom: God, that's . . .

CARTER: Yeah, It's whatever, but . . .] this once, in the grocery store, we're at an Albertsons and pushing *four* baskets around—you wanna know how humiliating that shit is?—and I'm supposed to be at a game by seven, I'm on JV, and she's just farting around in the candy aisle, picking up bags of "fun-size" Snickers and checking out the *calories*. Yeah. I mean, what is that?! So, I suddenly go off on her, like, this sophomore in high school, but I'm all screaming in her face. . . . "Don't look at the package, take a look in the fucking *mirror*, you cow!! PUT 'EM DOWN!" Holy shit, there's stock boys—bunch of guys I know, even—are running down the aisle. Manager stumbling out of his glass booth there, the works. (*Beat.*) But you know what? She doesn't say a word about it. Ever. Not about the swearing, the things I called her, nothing. Just this, like, one tear I see . . . as we're sitting at a stoplight on the way home. That's all.

[Tom: Wow. I'm, I mean . . .]

CARTER: I did feel that way, though. Maybe I shouldn't've yelled or . . . but it was true, what I said. You don't like being fat, there's a pretty easy remedy, most times. Do-not-jam-so-much-food-in-your-fucking-gullet. (*Beat.*) It's not that hard.

FEAR ITSELF, SECRETS OF THE WHITE HOUSE

BY JEAN-CLAUDE VAN ITALLIE

A cruelly dysfunctional family in the White House results in a cruelly dysfunctional national policy.

SCENE
At the White House, General Attorney Sing Sing, *a Southern revivalist preacher in a black suit, delivers a eulogy for one of the Emperor's children. The eulogy turns into a ferocious call to arms.*

TIME
The reign of George W. Butch

General Attorney Sing Sing: (*Southern drawl, and a fire-and-brimstone preaching style.*) First, I want to offer my best condolences to our famous Emperor Butch and his beautiful Empress Mommy. I know how you're feeling, Emperor Butch and Mommy. Your little girl's hurt. But I say unto you, Sir, put your feelings behind you. Right now. It's time to move on and do your duty. The greatest emperors in the world flinched not in the face of duty. Bravely ignoring their feelings, in the name of righteous revenge they did pillage and burn and torture and kill. They did. And now it's your turn, Emperor Butch. Your turn to demonstrate your toughness to the world, to become part of this empire's glory. History will praise and uplift you to the heaven of everlasting fame, Emperor Butch, for girding up your powerful loins and battening down your iron guts to lead us forward into righteous battle against evil, lest our enemy think for one single solitary second he could attack us first. Our Father who art in heaven, the Lord God did command the slaughter of Jerusalem, saying, "Cut down the old men, the young men, the young women, and the little children—and the old women. No peace for the wicked. Cry aloud. Spare not the rod. Lift up your voice as a scourge." Thus did Our Father who art in Heaven, the Lord God, thus did he command: "I will turn my almighty hand against the little ones. So sound now the trumpets and march ye forth in the whirlwind. For behold, I shall rise up like a shining scimitar and turn my sharp blade against those who threaten to rise up against me. I shall execute vengeance upon the heathen for I am a destroying wind. So make bright the arrows, gather the shields and prepare the ambush. Babylon's sins reek unto heaven! Her plagues shall come, and punishments upon her people—death, mourning and famine, and she shall be utterly burned in fire!"

FÊTES DE LA NUIT
BY CHARLES MEE

The play examines love and passion. In the monologue HENRY *talks to a young woman* HE *has just met.*

Or make of the monologue any character in any circumstance you like.

SCENE
Where else? In Paris.

TIME
Today

HENRY:
    I wonder:
    would you marry me
    or
    would you have a coffee with me
    and think of having a conversation
    that would lead to marriage?

    If not right now
    maybe later this evening?

Or late supper.
Or breakfast tomorrow
or lunch or tea in the afternoon
or a movie
or dinner the day after
Thursday for lunch
or Friday dinner
or perhaps you would go for the weekend with me
to my parents' home in Provence
or we could stop along the way
and find a little place for ourselves
to be alone.

Or just we could
have coffee over and over again
every day
until we get to know one another
and we have the passage of the seasons
in the café
we could celebrate our anniversary
and then perhaps you would forget
that you are not married to me
and we can have a child.

Because
don't you think
after we have been together for a year
it will be time to start to think of these things?

You know, I have known many women.
I mean, I don't mean to say . . .
I mean just
you know
my mother, my grandmother

my sisters
and also women I have known romantically
and then, too, friends,
and even merely acquaintances
but you know
in life
one meets many people
and it seems to me
we know so much of another person
in the first few moments we meet
not from what a person says alone
but from the way they hold their head
how they listen
what they do with their hand as they speak
or when they are silent
and years later
when these two people break up
they say
I should have known from the beginning
in truth
I did know from the beginning
I saw it in her, or in him
the moment we met
but I tried to repress the knowledge
because it wasn't useful at the time
because,
for whatever reason
I just wanted to go to bed with her as fast as I could
or I was lonely
and so I pretended I didn't notice
even though I did
exactly the person she was from the first moment
I knew
and so it is with you

and I think probably it is the same for you with me
we know one another
right now from the first moment
we know so much about one another in just this brief time
and we have known many people
and for myself
I can tell
you are one in a million
and I want to marry you
I want to marry you
and have children with you
and grow old together
so I am begging you
just have a coffee with me.

FOLKDANCE
BY ROBIN REESE

GLENN *is a 16-year-old African-American man who just jumped into the window of a neighbor, whom* HE *has never met before.* HE*'s cut and bleeding. His father is out looking for him and* GLENN *is quite scared for his life.* HE*'s telling the neighbor, Jessica, a 30-something Jewish woman, as well as Moisha, a 50-something African-American Ph.D., and Carlos, a 30-something Puerto Rican Chinese-delivery man, his story.*

SCENE
Jessica's apartment

TIME
The present

GLENN: When my dad came in and saw us, she had been laughing at me. I was naked, lying on the bed, limp, and she was laughing at me and calling me a girly-boy and telling me I was only half a man, not like my father, and that I was a queer and lots of mean stuff, and my dad walked in and heard all this. That's why he punched me the first time. It's like he forgot all about my sleeping with his girlfriend, and then it was all about me being gay. And today he got me out of bed and told me that we were going out. He wanted me to go sleep with some whores. He said maybe Randy wasn't the best thing going, but he knew other girls that would make me hard and who I could have sex with, only he said really bad, gross things, that I won't repeat because it would offend Jess.

We were out, driving to this one girl's house, and I told him I wouldn't go and if he made me then I'd tell Mom about his girlfriend, and he said that no I wouldn't because he'd tell her that I was a faggot and then I said, no he wouldn't because she was the one who came up to me and said that she knew I was different and that I probably didn't like girls, and if I wanted to go love men, that was fine with her, she wouldn't love me any less. And that got me thinking about things, and I realized that she was right. I was gay and if my mom loved me, that's okay. But then Randy came up to me at school and she told me that I was good lookin' and she wanted to spend some time with me and she started rubbin' her body on me.

If I had been alone, I would've told her no thank you, but wouldn't have insulted her, maybe lied that I already had a girl, or something, but this was in front of my boys, and she's a cutie, so I had to go with it, like I was interested. And by going along with it, I thought maybe my mom was wrong, maybe I just hadn't met the right girl, and she was the right girl — she had been the right girl for a lot of guys, so I thought, okay, I'll give it a try. What's there to lose?

FOLKDANCE
BY ROBIN REESE

MOISHA *is a 50-something African-American professor with a Ph.D. in Religion, who speaks in a fake British accent.* HE *lives in the same building as 30-something Jessica, who just buried her father.* MOISHA *walks in on Jessica, clearly distraught, in the arms of Carlos, a young Puerto Rican man* MOISHA *has never seen before. At Jessica's request,* MOISHA *is telling Carlos his story.*

SCENE
Jessica's apartment

TIME
The present

MOISHA: So . . . as I had been in the midst of telling you, I grew up in New Jersey. It's quite boring in New Jersey, and darling . . . that's an understatement. Anyhoo . . . I came up during a time when, in addition to going to church, my momma would take me to NAACP family mixers. In the sixties she became heavily involved with the Black Power movement and started going to an African-inspired church. My parents changed their names to Adowa and Ali. They tried to make me answer to Jawara but I'm not some dog they brought home from the pound, already named, but willing to come when called by anything, just to have a home and food. I had different ideas for myself, and like the flower children in the Vietnam era, I decided to live my own life, so I became Jewish, and changed my name to Moisha, and so I started looking for who I really wanted to be. I thought—if they can reinvent themselves, then I could too, but I'd be in control. During our senior-year field trip, one of the new teachers took us to New York. My friend Clay and I went up to Harlem. We weren't supposed to, but Clay was interested in seeing what the real black folk were up to. My mom told me I should really go to Harlem, instead of all the "white shit" UN they were taking us to. We were walking around and I saw this little place and heard this music in a language I'd never heard before. We went in and there was this Black guy wearing this white robe with tassels, and he had a big unkempt beard, and he was singing in this language, he had this black box on his head and the straps were around his arm. It turned out that I was witnessing Rabbi Matthew conduct a Bar Mitzvah class for a small group of 12-year-old boys, Black boys, like me, who were going to be Bar Mitzvahed later that week. He had been chanting in Hebrew. It just felt right. I met Rabbi Matthew, who was with the Commandment Keepers in Harlem. Boy, did that man move me, so I became a Jew. I moved to the City to go to City University, where I studied Religion and eventually took a Ph.D. Darling, it was a type of paradise. All my Jersey brothers and sisters were being beaten and taken off to jail, several were killed, but me, I was holed up in one of these library cubbyholes with my yarmulke on, and I would learn with the hip Jewish kids who'd dared to study with a Black brother. I studied the Talmud and Maimonides, and took my degrees with pride. The worst part of being Black in the sixties was that people would call me a kike and knock the yarmulke off my head.

FREEDOM HIGH

BY ADAM KRAAR

HENRY, 26, *an African-American man, has been working for the civil rights movement for the past three years. Although training the volunteers at a college in Ohio,* HE *struggles with doubts about the project.* HE'S *also grieving over his brother, who was severely beaten by white racists. In this speech,* HENRY *opens up to Jessica, a young white volunteer with whom* HE'S *become involved.*

SCENE
The front seat of Jessica's car, parked in a lot at Western College in Ohio

TIME
Summer 1964

HENRY: You don't! Just shut it. You don't understand. . . . See . . . before they got to my brother, they had me. I was canvassing some farmers outside town, and took a shortcut through the woods. Suddenly I was surrounded by the . . . reddest of rednecks I ever seen. They were pink with anger, 'cause they heard some Freedom Niggers were talkin' to their colored folk. Five of 'em, with bicycle chains and a big pipe. One of 'em had this big wad of pink bubble gum he kept poppin'.

(*Pause.*)

So you know what I did? Jessica? I pretended like I was somebody's cousin, like I was just some sharecropper, payin' a visit from the next county. Started sayin' all this bull jive like . . . "No, suh, I, I, I don't want to get involved in no politics. My family's a good family, we works for Mr. Reed over in Florence, Mr. Reed good to us, we never want no trouble, no suh!" I'm bowin' and movin' my head around like a wooden puppet, and cryin' . . .

(*Pause.*)

I'd been beaten before, shot at, jailed in the night. But somethin' happened that day. . . . Suddenly, didn't wanna die, not like that. They bought my story, and let me go, with just a kick to my pants. But later, those crackers find out who I really am, and come after me. They come to Mabley, and grab my brother off the street. Friend of the family saw it. "We know who you are, nigger. You takin' a ride with us."

Thought he was me!

GAP

BY CAROL LASHOF

AARON, *a high school senior with focus issues, addresses his teachers regarding his difficulties with his studies despite his best efforts, especially regarding the dreaded homework.*

SCENE
A large public high school in a progressive American city

TIME
The present

AARON: Dear teachers: This is the beginning of my last year of high school. I would like it to be wonderful. More likely it will not be. More likely it will be awful. That's just a guess, but an educated guess, based on past experience. Not that I blame teachers. I love teachers. Some of them. My first-grade teacher for instance. I still send her a birthday card.

No. I blame homework. I hate homework. And teachers who won't give you extra time if you need it. And talking in class — because I'm a nervous wreck. Also group projects. I really, really hate group projects. You see, I used to get stuck doing all the work. Now I just refuse to do any at all. Either way, it's not so good. I know that.

My relationships with my peers are problematic. You don't need to point it out. I am fully aware of the fact. My relationships with my parents are likewise problematic. I don't think I'll go into that right now. The point being — teachers are actually the least of my worries. Except you give so much homework.

In first grade we didn't get homework. Well, maybe sometimes we had to write in a notebook or draw pictures but the spelling didn't matter and my teacher always wrote me a nice note which my parents would read to me since I couldn't read yet, and then it was like not just my teacher was praising me but also my mom or dad was saying, "I love your funny picture of the pumpkin" — or whatever. And a couple of times we had to memorize a poem and I didn't even mind reciting it in front of the class, because I loved the poem, like this one:

Fly away, fly away, over the sea,
Sun-loving swallow, for summer is done.
Come again, come again, come back to me,
Bringing the summer and bringing the sun.

It's not that I don't try to do my homework. I come straight home from school. I mean, what else would I do? I don't like "extracurricular activities" and I don't like "hanging out with the guys" and I for sure don't have a girlfriend. So I come home. And I don't watch TV because TV is stupid. I just sit right down at the dining room table and I take out my books and sharpen my pencils and I look at the list of things I have to do and I think, this isn't so bad, what's the big deal? And I think, today will be the day when I finish my homework on time, I'll even finish it before my parents get home, and they won't yell at me and I won't be stressed out, and after dinner I'll listen to some maybe John Coltrane or Santana and I'll go to bed at ten and tomorrow I'll be rested and cheerful and I'll turn in all my homework and the rest of my life will be happy, and maybe I'll even get a girlfriend.

But that's not how things turn out.

GAP
BY CAROL LASHOF

An African-American sophomore in high school, WILL *struggles with being racially typecast instead of being placed in the more advanced courses that would challenge and interest* HIM.

SCENE
A large public high school in a progressive American city

TIME
The present

WILL: I have this dream where I go back to my grade-school playground and I say to the other Black boys: Am I Black enough for you now? Am I? Black enough?

Kindergarten, first grade, second, third, it was always Sophie Rosen and me at the top of the class and best friends. Math: when the other kids were doing drill-and-kill arithmetic problems, row after row, we got to sit in the hallway with a book of logic games, like figuring out if you told your parents you'd wash the dishes for just a penny on the first day and then double it every day—by the end of week three you'd be making more than $10,000. Sophie and me, we figured out by the time we were ten, we'd be billionaires. Then we got the giggles trying to decide how we'd spend all that money, and the teacher across the hall got mad about the noise and sent us back to our classroom and complained to Mr. Theodore about letting us be on our own in the hallway. But he kept on letting us anyway, because he was chill. And he liked us, he trusted us—I could tell.

The third-grade spelling bee: down to the wire. Sophie spelled "orangutan." I spelled "Connecticut," remembering the capital "C." We both messed up on "vivacious." She beat me on "rhythm." Ironic, huh?

This school is so big, if something gets screwed up, you can grow old and die trying to fix it. For instance, last year, in ninth grade, they put me in Algebra I instead of Algebra II—and by the time I got moved to the right class I was way behind and the teacher was pissed off about having to deal with me. He didn't think I belonged there—I could tell.

This year, my classes are mostly so boring I don't see the point of going. No one notices whether I'm there or not anyway. There's a computer that's supposed to call home when you're absent, but mostly I can erase the messages before my parents get home.

I'm 6'2" and I have a buzz cut with "W" shaved into the back. Sometimes I see Sophie crossing the park on the way to school. She always waves and smiles, but her friends, they look at me and they just see "scary." I guess I'm Black enough for them.

GEM OF THE OCEAN

BY AUGUST WILSON

CITIZEN BARLOW, *a young man from Alabama in spiritual turmoil, recalls the tryst* HE *had with a woman and the loneliness that has ensued since.*

SCENE
The Hill District, Pittsburgh, Pennsylvania, in the parlor of Eli, Aunt Ester and Black Mary's home at 1839 Wylie Avenue

TIME
1904

CITIZEN: You got on that blue dress. I met this gal at a dance one time had on a blue dress. She had on a blue dress and she had her hair slicked back. Her mouth made her face look pretty. She was dancing and she had tears in her eyes. I asked her why she was crying. She said she was lonesome. I told her I couldn't fix that but if she wanted somebody to walk her home after the dance I'd walk her. See that she got home safe. She thanked me and went on crying. Say she felt better, and after the dance I could walk her home since I was going that way. She had a good time dancing with some of the other men. I danced with her some more. She was smiling but she still had tears in her eyes. After the dance I walked her home. I seen at the dance that she had a nice way about her. When she was walking home she put her hand in mine. She asked me did I want to stay the night. I told her yes. I told her I was at the dance looking for a woman. She asked me why didn't I tell her, we could have saved each other some time. I woke up in the morning and she was laying there crying. I didn't ask her about it. I didn't try and stop her. I lay there a while trying to figure out what to do. I ended up holding her in my arms. She started crying some more. I held her a while and then I left. I said good-bye to her and started walking away. She was standing in the door. I looked back and she was standing so she fit right in the middle of the door. I couldn't see if she was crying. She kind of waved at me. I got a little further on and turned and looked back and she was still there. Look like she had got smaller like she might have sat down in the doorway. That's what it looked like to me. I can still see her standing there. Had a green door and I can see her standing in it. I don't know what happened to her. I'd like to look on her face again. Just to know that she all right and if she stopped crying. If I could see her face I believe that would be enough.

[**BLACK MARY:** Maybe you'll get the chance. What you gonna tell her if you see her again?]

CITIZEN: I don't know. Sometimes I lay awake at night when I be lonely and ask myself what I would say to her. Sometimes I tell her to stop being lonely. I tell her it's something she doing to herself. But then I'm laying there lonely too and I have to ask myself was it something I was doing to myself? I don't know. I ain't lonely now. I ain't got no woman but I still don't feel lonely. I feel all filled up inside. That's something I done to myself. So maybe I did make myself lonely.

GEM OF THE OCEAN

BY AUGUST WILSON

CAESAR, *a successful Black man in his 50s, explains his difficult past and the importance of family to his younger sister.*

SCENE
The Hill District, Pittsburgh, Pennsylvania, in the parlor of Eli, Aunt Ester and Black Mary's home at 1839 Wylie Avenue.

TIME
1904

CAESAR: I got to play the hand that was dealt to me. You look around and see you black. You look at the calendar. Slavery's over. I'm a free man. I can get up whatever time I want to in the morning. I can move all over and pick any woman I want. I can walk down the street to the store and buy anything my money will buy. There ain't nothing I can't have. I'm starting out with nothing so I got to get a little something. A little place to start. You look and see the race you got to run is different than somebody else's. Maybe it's got more hills. It's longer. But this is what I got. Now what to do with it?

I look around and see where niggers got to eat and niggers got to sleep. I say if I had some bread I'd be a rich man. I got some bread. In the valley of the blind the one-eyed man is king. I started selling hoecakes off the back of a wagon. I'd cook them over the coals. I got me some beans. Selling them right out the pot. I even put a little pork in them. Police ran me off the corner. Say I needed a license. It took me a while but I got me a license. I had to pay six or seven people but I got me a license.

Niggers say my bowls was too small. I got bigger bowls. Say I didn't put enough pork in the beans. I put in more pork. I got me some chickens. I charged extra for the big ones and the people got mad. One man told me the chickens had big feet but they didn't have big wings. I seen I was in the wrong business. Said I was gonna let niggers eat on their own and give them a place to sleep. Only I didn't have no money to buy no property.

Went down to the bank to borrow some money. They told me I needed some collateral. Say you need something to borrow money against. I say all right, I'll get me some collateral. I opened me up a gambling joint in the back of the barbershop. Sold whiskey. The police closed it down. I had to put some bullet holes in a couple of niggers and the police arrested me. Put me on the county farm. I had to bust a couple of niggers upside the head for trying to steal my food. A couple tried to escape. I caught them. That don't do nothing but make it harder on everybody. They out there enjoying their freedom ducking and dodging the law and everybody else on half rations and got to make up their work.

A fellow named John Hanson started a riot. I seen that wasn't gonna be nothing but bad news. I took him on one-to-one. Man-to-man. He busted my eye. He busted my eye but I put down the riot. They gave me a year. I did six months when the mayor called me in to see him. Say he wanted to put me in charge of the Third Ward. Told me say you fry the little fish and send the big fish to me. They give me a gun and a badge. I took my badge and gun and went down to the bank and laid it on the counter. Told them I wanted to borrow some money on that. There was a fellow name Harry Bryant had a place on Colwell Street he sold me. They ran him out of town. Charged me three times what it was worth. Took the money and ran. They tried to kill him for selling to a Negro. I say all right I got me a little start. Niggers got mad at me. Said I must have thought I was a white man 'cause I got hold to a little something. They been mad at me ever since. Everybody mad at me. You mad at me.

[**Black Mary:** It ain't about being mad at you, Caesar. You're my brother. I respect and honor that. I always have and I always will. But we don't owe each other any more than that.]

Caesar: I ain't got but one sister and I try to do right by her and you push me away. Family is important. I know the value of family. Blood is thicker than water. It's been that way and always will be. You can't even water it down.

Your mother wanna turn blood into vinegar. When Uncle Jack was dying she wouldn't even go see him. Say he was fooling the people being a fake blind man. She was right. But that's her brother! He deserve better than that. You can't sit in judgment over people. That's God's job. God decide who done right or wrong. Uncle Jack dying and calling for his sister and she wouldn't even go and see him. That's the kind of mother you got. You let her run your life. Got you thinking like her. You thinking wrong and don't even know it. Many a time I tried to make up to her but she wouldn't have it. Called me a scoundrel. But that didn't stop me from paying for her funeral. I paid for the funeral and even shed a few tears. If I had known any prayers I would have said them. Why? 'Cause she family. You give up on family and you ain't got nothing left.

GONE MISSING

BY STEVEN COSSON AND THE CIVILIANS

The play was created from interviews with real people about lost objects. The DANCER *is an exuberant young guy, lively, fast-talking and sometimes explosive.* HE *seems like someone who might be a DJ or plays in a band, and it's a little surprise when the audience finds out that* HE*'s a dancer.* HE*'s talking to his interviewer, who is a close friend.*

SCENE
New York City

TIME
The present

DANCER: I left my cell phone in the cab when I got out. So later — I was soooo exhausted, so I just totally spaced on the phone, you know? — I called the number later, when I got home and nothing and I called and called and called and I just kept getting voice mail voice mail you know? Then finally the phone picks up and I hear these girls talking in the background, you know. This one girl is like, "Girl, you and that stupid phone you found" or something, and I could hear rustling and stuff because the phone was in her pocket or something and so I started screaming, you know, I was like (*Cupping his hands around his mouth and whispering a scream.*) Heeeeeey!!! HeeeeeeeeeeeeeY! Hellooooooooooooo! You know and I was making all this high-pitched noise you know, so she would hear me so I'm like ooooooooooooooooooo! OOOOOOOOOOOOOOOO! Heeeeeeeeyyyyyyyyyyy!!! This is my phone HEEEEEEEEEEEY! And I am so fucking exhausted dude. I'm just so tired. Heeeeeeeeyyyy! And then I hear it just like rustled and shut off. And I'm like FAAACK! I had this image of these two girls fucking hanging out in Central Park, walking through the park in school uniforms with my phone in their backpack. . . . No, they're not sexy, just, you know . . . regular school uniforms and I mean this image is soo clear to me. And I'm like FAAACK! And I call back and they don't answer. So a couple of days later or something I try again and this woman answers and I'm like HELLO HELLO, This is my phone and I lost it in a cab please don't hang up! And she was like, "Yeah, I just got out of this rehearsal . . . I'm a dancer. Do you know where Capezio's is?" you know, and I was like, "I'm a dancer too." So she left it for me at Capezio's. Oh and the worst part of this whole story is that two hours after I got it from Capezio's, I was fucking running up the stairs and I tripped and fucking cracked the whole phone. It was in my pocket and I — my hip landed on it and broke it. I had a huge fucking bruise.

HEIRLOOM
BY ANDY BRAGEN

A young MAN *meets up with his ex-girlfriend to return her belongings.*

SCENE
Union Square Park, New York City, near the thrice-weekly farmers' market. A series of benches are visible. A young MAN *with a duffel, and a plastic bag full of vegetables* HE *has just purchased, addresses a woman on a bench.*

TIME
A midsummer afternoon. The present.

MAN: So I guess I'll start with an apology. A blanket apology. We can get into specifics as we go along. There are specifics I know, long-seated matters that . . . anyway . . .

(HE *holds up a tomato.*)

Straight from the Farmers' Market. Consider it a peace offering. Want a bite? You sure? Your loss.

(HE *takes a bite out of the tomato.*)

They call these heirlooms, meaning they haven't been crossbred into red tasteless oblivion. Not so pretty, and not so durable, no good for trucking in from Mexico, but texturous and tasty, a tomato worth the money—I made a pitcher of gazpacho the other day—remember my gazpacho? This one was twice as good as usual—really incredible flavor—I used the super-ripe ones from the bottom box—only a buck a pound after 5PM—if we stick around for a bit we can buy some—quite a savings. I would've made you a batch if you'd come by, but with you insisting on a "neutral location," and me having to lug this duffel, well, I wasn't as inclined as usual to sacrifice my Tupperware.

Mother was asking about you—I said that as far as I know you're well, and she responded "as far as you know?" and I said well, yes, that's right, truth is we're not exactly speaking, that truth being, truth be told, a kind of a white lie since I am in fact speaking, right now, as we speak, but of course you, bless your black heart, are here, and that does count for something. I guess.

Speaking of textures, I ironed your clothes. Folded them too. Socks, underwear, bras, skirts, tops—everything, starched, folded and ironed. I was careful and thorough, lingering—it took me half the night. Very educational—sometimes I iron my own, but it's just a quick pass-over, kind of like my cooking, just good enough, but nothing worth sharing, but when you're doing it for someone else—I think you'll be happy.

About those calls—I do want to apologize—they weren't necessarily intentional, which is not to say that they were unintentional, but rather that I got a bit ahead of myself. Two years from now, when all of this will be forgotten and enough assholes will have passed through your life that your memory of me will be almost fond, that will perhaps be a better moment to call—and I assure you I will call, from wherever I may be. But

I suppose that now it's not entirely appropriate, right, though truth is, knowing you, even though it was 3AM, I am SURE that you were up, watching the phone as it rang, and I know you knew that it was me, suffering, in grave despair, and for you to ignore such a plea is, to my mind, well, callous. Carrot?

(HE *munches on the carrot.*)

Tasty — you sure you don't want a snack? You can never eat enough carrots. And then of course there's the other night — and apologies are due for that too — he looked like a nice fellow — strong — though maybe a bit old for you, I saw the bald spot, and even from the doorframe I could smell his feet — anyway, here are the keys — last copy I swear it.

You can keep mine — it's okay. Though like Mother always used to say, best if you call first, as you never know, you really never do know, what with all this organic food, me too, I could be strong too. Thanks are due to you for this — you who taught me the difference between kale, chard, and collards — and now — as I'm sure you can see from my skin tone, those complex nutrients course through my veins. Here, feel my texturous arm. My blood is racing. And maybe it's the leafy greens or maybe it's you — cause you still do affect me — your scowl, your tapping foot, your light sheen of sweat — I love your sweat, always have. Don't worry, soon enough it'll be cool — the day, it will pass, the week, the month, summer, the year, two years, and then your phone will ring — happy birthday, I'll sing. Happy birthday. Pick up this time, okay?

IMAGINE

BY REBECCA BASHAM

DAVID, *a man in his 40s, speculates about assassinations after attending a political address.* HE *looks like an investment banker — very prim, proper and pulled together.*

SCENE
A cocktail party

TIME
The present

DAVID: Have you ever thought about an assassination? I mean, have you ever really thought about it? We've heard the poetry, the sound bites, the memories of JFK — a whole generation remembers exactly what they were doing, exactly the moment that those black-and-white impressions of a life ending zoomed their way into houses and hearts— We've heard their voices: *I was at school; I was at work; I was cooking; I was, I was, I was.* We've heard death knells through the memories of our predecessors and their cameras whirring, always whirring, *I have a dream,* and then sleep came too soon. I was 13 and John Lennon was 40. He was shot outside the Dakota on the Upper West Side. Manhattan — so much a part of American mythology to millions who've never seen it. His was a life imagined; a life ending wrongly, unjustly.

And we can hear them, participants in all of these lives gone from us, their voices questioning, *Who could have? Why did it come to this? How can we live in a world where?* And I was always one of those voices—*wrong to take a life*—so surely, so concretely. Until now. Why has no one even tried? He's there—sneaking into our homes through digital encoding, pouring through the drains, sweeping under the door through the cracks as surely as the germs he uses to frighten us, grinning that shit-eating grin in our faces as if to taunt us— He's taunting us. I've never killed. I've never been unstable. I've never even considered owning a gun or any kind of a weapon. I never thought I could even think about killing. But I do. Each and every time I hear his voice lying to me, to everyone—every time I hear another sentence lead to murder, lead to hatred, lead to ignorance—every time, I wonder why no one has done it yet—hasn't even attempted—it's been done before. Think about it.

THE IMPOSSIBILITY
OF MOST THINGS
BY ALBERT INNAURATO

In the scene from which this monologue is taken, MICHAEL CRENSHAW *meets the love of his life, a girl named Golda (he will change her name). In the play* HE *is a man in his mid-40s, although here, because it is a memory play,* MICHAEL *is in his teens.* HE *and Golda (who wants to write) are trading theatre-in-the-schools stories.*

SCENE
The Freshman Orientation Mixer at Harvard

TIME
The early seventies

(MICHAEL *listens to a pop ballad.*)

MICHAEL: Strange the power of cheap music. Is that Cole Porter or Noël Coward? But then is there a difference? I was almost in *Private Lives* once. Not at Groton where I was enrolled. You see, Golda — oh, that name, let me tremble un peu! (HE *trembles theatrically.*) We might have to change that. My slightly younger sibling, Cynthia, was at Andover. The Drama Teacher there, Mr. Shingles, was doing *Private Lives.* Thirty-six women auditioned. No genital males did. I determined to try out. True actors are hungry! We were between plays at Groton. And Groton, you see, ill-fated Groton, is a bastion of the higher stand-up-comedy type writing of, say, Neil (not Noël) Simon. So I hitchhiked to Andover. You know:

(*Sings a bit from the Janis Joplin hit* "Me and Bobby McGee.")

Janis Joplin is just like Callas, only hoarser. I met her once. She threw up on me. I was thrilled. At Andover, I auditioned for Mr. Shingles, fat and hysterical, not entirely my style. Later he was fired and sent to jail for binding the hockey team in Saran Wrap. Don't ask. Of course, I got the part. In fact, I got both male parts. Cynthia was cast in both female parts. It would be an early post-modern *Private Lives* with intimations of incest. But one of her classmates, a jealous girl named Wysteria Wicket . . . I'm serious, why do you laugh? Do you think perhaps I'm Ivy Compton-Burnett in preppy drag? (*Back to his story.*) Wysteria Wicket turned me in. I claimed asylum as a political refugee from Groton. I was returned there for disciplinary action. I was barred from all Neil Simon plays for the foreseeable future. Later, as we were watching my father and younger brother play tennis while my beloved sister watched and wept—Dada wouldn't play with girls—my mother said to me: "You are a disgrace, Michael Crenshaw, a noisy, unpopular scamp. And since Dada plans to disinherit you, you may well need Neil Simon or equivalent to live as an actor." "You know, Mama," I replied, "though I realize Neil Simon is the only commercial playwright we have in the foreseeable future of these early seventies, I feel confident that TV-type writing will lose its power, that a society in which most people have gone to college and fought for civil rights and objected to pointless slaughter and illegal bombings in a far-off place called Vietnam, will transcend that type of entertainment and start to value the arts." Her eyes teared, she squeezed her face shut. She sneezed. Hay fever.

JIMMY JIM JIM AND THE M.F.M.

BY MERON LANGSNER

Manipulative without being malicious and suffering perhaps from a bit of a Napoleonic complex, JIMMY JIM JIM *is trying to comfort his friend, the* M.F.M., *who has been arrested after participating in a violent bar fight.*

SCENE
The visiting room of the county penitentiary

TIME
The present

JIMMY JIM JIM: You hanging in there, Machine? You're looking a lot better.

You still look like shit, but it's better than the last time I saw you.

I mean, you wake up fucked up locked up locked down beat down and hung over an you just wanna get out go out go home kick back and watch the game but you got shit to deal with, am I right? Am I right?

They treatin you all right in here? As well as can be expected I mean.

I don't suppose you remember the other night much.

One of your blackouts. Shit.

I dunno what the public defender asshole told you. He looks like a dick by the way. I seen it all though.

Course I seen it all, I was there wit you.

It was like this. We come into the place and we're drinkin, cause it's Friday. It's Friday so we're drinkin the good stuff. Heineken. No, no Friday was a few days ago. They didn't tell you much at all, did they? Fucked up I tell you. But back to the bar.

They announce there's gonna be fightin and we ignore it. Be cool to watch though.

You remember that right? Right?

Then they say, five hundred bucks.

Five hundred bucks is a lot of Heineken.

And more than that, guys are pulling out their paychecks and placin bets.

So we're drinkin. And we're thinking.

Five hundred bucks.

People are placin bets and I'm thinkin. Why not put my boy's talents to use, right? I mean, five hundred bucks. I stand up and say, "We call my boy here The M.F.M. That's short for The Motha Fuckin *Machine*. We used call him just The Machine, but it did not do him justice."

I'm workin the crowd.

And you sign up to fight.

I say to the guys in the bar, "The Motha Fuckin Machine . . . runs on tequila." We're drinkin free now so signing you up is already paying off.

You drink a *lot* of tequila, Machine.

You should watch that you know. Don't get mad, Machine. Gettin mad gets you where you are today. I'm tryin to help you out, y'know? Like advice. Yeah. Advice.

And now it's time.

They got a ring set up in the middle of the bar. I guess they do this a lot.

I doubt they'll ever do it again though.

It's your turn. We have another shot of tequila for good luck.

I don't know anymore, Machine. Maybe we shouldn't have done it.

Looks like you're fightin Joe College. What the fuck is this kid doin out here? He's even got a fuckin Harvard sweatshirt on. Well fuck 'im, he wants to come out and play wit the big boys, let 'im.

I offer him a shot of tequila. You know, sportsmanship.

Says he doesn't drink.

Joe College asshole.

Can you see out of that eye yet, Machine? He got you pretty good that first time.

He pulled that Bruce Van Damme Lee shit. Men ain't supposed to spread their legs like that. It ain't natural. I never seen that before.

I never seen the Mother Fucking Machine go down before either.

You're down. And the kid is dancing. Dancing. Like Muhammed Ali bouncing around.

Then you get back up.

He's dancing.

He tries that Ginsu Jinsu crap again.

That don't last long.

You musta broke his nose that time. I dunno what else.

He goes down. I think it's done.

Then. It's the scariest thing I ever saw.

He gets up.

Crying.

And he's on his feet swinging on the Mother Fucking Machine and sobbing like a baby.

Kid had balls. I give him that.

You're both on the ground. And then the Machine is on top of him and he ain't movin.

He's still breathin, but he ain't movin.

'Cept when you hit 'im.

He's done.

You didn't have to keep hittin him, Machine.

It's the tequila. I seen that happen to you before. But never like that. Blackout. You don't even remember, do you? Do you?

You did not have to keep hittin him.

Don't get mad, Machine. I'm tryin to help you. Like I said. Advice.

The kid woke up in the hospital and says he ain't pressing charges. Sportsmanship. His parents' lawyer says different though. They're moving him to a hospital in the city today they said. Reconstructive surgery. The hospital here wasn't good enough for them.

I dunno, Machine.

You didn't have to keep hittin him.

I gotta go.

I'll check in on Beth for ya.

The guys all say hi.

Most of em anyway.

I'll see you next week, Machine.

Don't take any shit from any of the assholes in here.

You hang in there.

JOHNNY'S GOT A GUN

BY JOHN FLECK

JOHN, *an actor, enters with a stuffed toy pony and places it on the other side of a make-believe bed onstage.*

SCENE
Los Angeles

TIME
Now

JOHN: I had a Dream! It was a couple of years ago . . . my partner and me — we'd been together thirteen years. Here we are, two bohemian artists and all of a sudden I start doin' TV and overnight we're living in this big-ass house in the Los Feliz hills where everything is big, including the new king-size bed we're sleepin' in . . . with that king-size gulf between us and he's leaving me. I'm getting the pink slip — he got a job in NYC at the Guggenheim, and he's checkin' out in a few days and I'm freakin' — the bombs are goin' off in my head . . . so I take a marinol capsule. You know what marinol is? I was on a river-rafting trip, and all my pals were doin' marinol (it's a marijuana extract), but I wanted to live, so I said can I take this later to help me fall asleep? And they said sure . . . so this is the rainy day I take my marinol — gulp — and

I zonk right out—sleeping heavy and then three hours later . . . hear it . . .

(*A little boy's voice as Johnny.*) MA! Shhh! MA! (*Regular voice.*) And even though I'm still asleep, my eyes haven't opened that wide in years . . . and I hear this little boy's voice again, "MA! I'M SCARED." And I know right then and there it's me, Johnny, and I'm 7 years old on Settlement Acres Drive in Brookpark, Ohio. It's later that evening after the July 4th BBQ/talent show at the American Legion, and there's a thunderstorm raging outside . . . . I'm in bed, holdin' on to my Pony—I always slept with Pony and Mom's just crawled in beside me.

(*Using a woman's voice as Ma.*) He wouldn't bother me if I slept with the kids—

(*As Johnny.*) Dad's just come home from the Legion—he's drunk—he's down in the rec room and you can hear him slammin' doors and hitting the wall and and then I hear it.

(*A gunshot in distance.*)

(Johnny's *scared.*) Ma, he's got his gun—shhh! And then I hear—

(*Gunshot with glass breaking.*)

He just shot the TV. . . . MA, I'm scared. Shhh! He's gonna' blow my freakin' fag brains out, Ma . . . Ma!

(*As Ma.*) Shhh. Don't be scared. . . .

(Johnny's *voice.*) But Ma—

(*Repeat as Ma.*) Shhh, he can't hurt us if we stick together.

(*As Johnny.*) Hold on, Ma! — and it's me and Ma on Pony—all sticking together—I know how to get us outta here, Ma. Look (*Sings a snatch of the end of "I'm Flying" from the Broadway musical Peter Pan.*)—I'm flyin just like Peter Pan, up in the sky . . . and I look down at the bed at Ryan sleeping over on the other side of that giant king-size bed—and I say, "WHOA!!!" (*Whinny.*) "*Whoa!*"

Ma, can we take him with us, Ma? I wanna stick with him, too, Ma—I finally found me a man who loves me. He loves me so much, Ma, and he's never hurt me—he's an angel. He's so kind and pure and innocent. And Ryan's eyes open wide and he yells up at me, "STOP FETISHIZING ME! I'M REAL." (*John falls down to floor.*) And I come toppling back down onto earth into bed. (*Throws Pony onto the other side of the make-believe bed.*) And I realize I'm tripping my Goddamn brains out on marinol . . . and I look over at Ryan (*Uses pony as* Ryan.) and I get THE PICTURE. Yeah, you're "real," all right. He's twelve years younger than me, but he looks older than me, hair thinning, almost bald, blotchy skin on his cheeks—blackheads. Come on. No excuse. I do laser resurfacing—gets rid of veins and little wrinkle lines. It's called taking care of yourself. Ryan, too much nose hair and ear hair—hairy chest—nose crooked—his mouth open, drool dripping out onto the pillow—teeth just a lil' too stained and crooked. Look at my teeth. (*Warps his face into a big SMILE.*) I had braces put on ten years ago. I bleach once a month. There's no excuse for crooked, yellow teeth. REAL? Sorry, I DON'T WANT REAL!

LA TEMPESTAD

BY LARRY LOEBELL

In this modern adaptation of Shakespeare's The Tempest, CALIBAN *is a bartender/concierge/tour guide, a disgruntled employee of Prospero's museum on the Puerto Rican island of Vieques. American planes have just bombed the beach.*

SCENE
The beach at Vieques. CALIBAN *alone on the beach, his clothes in awful disarray. Broken palm branches cover* HIM.

TIME
Late 2002, just before the 2003 invasion of Iraq. It is morning; the sky is bright.

CALIBAN: Ohhh. Dreams, do not go. (*Covering his eyes.*) Shit. I am blinded awake. Where am I? What day is this? What is that light? Did I sleep here, in the open, under the stars? Oh, I hurt. What has turned my soothing sun to sadistic swordsman stabbing my eyes? I will stand. Survey. There. Nothing. But something. Itches. Nags. What? A flash of light, a cry. When was that? My head. Did I drink all of this? (*Examining the bottle.*) From Prospero's private reserve. I was working at the bar, I remember. (*A beat.*) Then there was a sound. What was it? A sudden squall? Thunder? *Don't be afraid*, I remember telling myself. The island is full of sounds and sweet airs that usually give delight. Sometimes a sound like a thousand tingling instruments hums in your ears. I do not think it was a storm. I am dry as toast, my clothes sand-streaked, not rain-splattered. What then? I think there were shouts. Were they shouts? Run. Run! RUN! And I was afraid then. Did I run? From what? From where? My head. Then, I remember, there was a flash and I was flying, a marionette, jerked upward by unseen hands, somersaulting over the scenery, a soaring angel swimming up the sky on a wave of heat. I remember near the top noticing this claret clenched in my fist and thinking, *I didn't pay for this.* (*Teetering. Head pounding.*) And then, in an instant, angelic puppet flight curtailed, I was condemned, discarded, plunged down to sand. The beach breaking my fall. Stumbling on my knees and thinking, *This is not right, this is not a thing a man can do, propelled into sky on no force other than wind.* And then there were the voices again, softer, anguished. But I couldn't move. Couldn't. And then crawling out of range of the heat, in the sudden darkness, where there was no sound but lapping water, and the breeze was the breeze of scented night, I sank down to the succor of sleep. (*A beat.*) Was there more than this? I must have dreamed the rain. The clouds, I dreamt, had opened and dropped their riches down on me, so much so that when I woke, I would cry to dream again.

THE LANGUAGE OF KISSES
BY EDMUND DE SANTIS

BLUE *is in his 20s, a simple attractive guy, slightly retarded. When* HE*'s unsure,* HE *has a nervous tic of ducking, as if someone were about to hit* HIM *on the head. His marriage proposal to Zan, a much older woman, has just been rejected.*

SCENE
A farm in Gideon, Ohio

TIME
June

BLUE: You were the first, Zan. You are the one! Now, you look at me! I swear. The first I let in. I was scared. I'm still scared. Any second I'm thinking. Wow. See. I. I. Ever since when I was little. I did a badsex thing. That's what she called it. My mom. One time we went up to Toledo to visit her brother, Uncle Jack. She was happy. She never went anywhere. We're goin' on some bus. She's talkin to everybody. She sings "You Are My Sunshine" over and over which I hate. But I'm glad she's in a good mood cause I'd hate to see what would happen if she got in a bad mood on a bus. We get there and there's a cousin. Kathy. Big for her age. Let's get alone in my room, she says. She's got this toy organ. With this cardboard to show colors. You follow the colors from the book. That's how you play songs. She tried to get me to play. Only I wasn't fast. She said you're an idiot you can't play it. Then she closes the door and starts to play. Soft first. Some song. Then louder. Crazier. Pounding. Not a song. Noise. I start jumpin around. She says, take your pants off. I did! My dinky's hard. It hurts even it's so hard. Stickin out. And Kathy's lookin at it. Poundin the keys harder yellin dance! makin sounds Indian whooping, I'm dancing around the room, my dinky's stickin out and it feels like it's getting harder and harder and . . . it's like I'm on the ceiling lookin down at myself, round and round . . . and . . . then . . . my mom comes in. She says Kathy get out of the room. She says she'll kill me if she ever sees me doin that again. Takin my dinky out in front of Kathy! Don't I know it's a sin cousins can't have sex. And my dinky's still stickin out, it won't go down. And the madder she gets the more it sticks out! She says put your pants on. My pants won't go over my dinky, it's stuck and it gets harder and she smacks it, and it gets harder I don't know why. Next thing I know she grabs a ruler off Kathy's desk, she hits it, over and over, this'll make you soft, this'll wilt that weeney, and just then Uncle Jack runs in to save the day and I . . . cried. (*Beat.*) Man that hurt. The ruler had one of them metal edges. It was twisted. It stuck out. It got me. I had five stitches. That's what the scar is. Near my—see I told you someday I'd tell you how I got the scar near my dinky, well, I always called it a dinky, that's probably not the right word to use, but. . . . (*Beat.*) When you touch me, when you touch my dinky, when you kiss me there—I know this is a goodsex thing.

THE LARAMIE PROJECT

BY MOISES KAUFMAN AND THE MEMBERS OF TECTONIC THEATER PROJECT

In 1998 in Laramie, Wyoming, student Matthew Shepard was beaten, tied to a barbed-wire fence, and left to die because he was gay. The Tectonic Theater Project traveled to Laramie and interviewed people in an attempt to understand the "incident" and the culture that allowed it. JEDEDIAH SCHULTZ, *one of those interviewed, is a 19-year-old university student.*

SCENE
A performance space with perhaps a table and chair

TIME
Late 1990s

JEDEDIAH SCHULTZ: I've lived in Wyoming my whole life. The family has been in Wyoming, well . . . for generations. Now when it came time to go to college, my parents can't—couldn't afford to send me to college. I wanted to study theater. And I knew that if I was going to go to college I was going to have to get on a scholarship—and so, uh, they have this competition each year, this Wyoming state high-school competition. And I knew that if I didn't take first place in, uh, duets, that I wasn't gonna get a scholarshp. So I went to the theater department of the university looking for good scenes, and I asked one of the professors—I was like, "I need—I need a killer scene," and he was like, "Here you go, this is it." And it was from *Angels in America*.

So I read it and I knew that I could win best scene if I did a good enough job.

And when the time came I told my mom and dad so that they would come to the competition. Now you have to understand, my parents go to everything—every ball game, every hockey game—everything I've ever done.

And they brought me into their room and told me that if I did that scene, that they would not come to see me in the competition. Because they believe that it is wrong—that homosexuality is wrong—they felt that strongly about it that they didn't want to come see their son do probably the most important thing he'd done to that point in his life. And I didn't know what to do.

I had never, ever gone against my parents' wishes. So I was kind of worried about it. But I decided to do it.

And all I can remember about the competition is that when we were done, me and my scene partner, we came up to each other and we shook hands and there was a standing ovation.

Oh, man, it was amazing! And we took first place and we won. And that's how come I can afford to be here at the university, because of that scene. It was one of the best moments of my life. And my parents weren't there. And to this day, that was the one thing that my parents didn't see me do.

And thinking back on it, I think, why did I do it? Why did I oppose my parents? 'Cause I'm not gay. So why did I do it? And I guess the only honest answer I can give is that, well, (HE *chuckles*.) I wanted to win. It was such a good scene; it was like the best scene!

Do you know Mr. Kushner? Maybe you can tell him.

THE LAST FREAK SHOW

BY PHILIP ZWERLING

At age 18, MONKEY-BOY, or BILL, who suffers from excessive body hair, has become the main attraction in a traveling freak show. After a performance, HE tells a young boy about his past and predicts great things for his future as the "Missing Link."

SCENE
A cage in front of a circus tent in Lubbock, in the Texas Panhandle

TIME
July 1933

(*The young man of 18 billed as "Monkey-Boy" lies in the bottom of the cage, which is covered in straw. HE rolls on his back and throws straw in the air. HE leaps to his feet, screams like a monkey and throws HIMSELF onto the bars, which HE clings to and thrashes wildly as if trying to pry them apart to escape. His clothes are ridiculously small for HIM. His pants end high above his ankles, his sleeves end above his wrists. His face and every visible area of his skin is covered with coarse hair. HE looks like a cross between an ape and a man. HE alternately throws back his head and howls, rolls on the floor of his cage, and rattles the bars. HE throws straw at the people HE sees beyond his cage. HE turns his back on the crowd and lowers his pants to seemingly show an entirely hairy rear end even as HE emits a crazy half laugh half howl. Again* HE *grabs the bars and makes monkey noises. Finally* HE *seems to watch as a crowd of people exits Stage Left. When* HE *thinks they are gone* HE *searches the bottom of his cage and finds a banana, which* HE *slowly peels and eats.* HE *spots someone, a young boy whom the audience does not see, who has stayed behind.* HE *hoots and howls at the child, considers continuing his act, and decides against it.* HE *offers the boy part of the banana by slowly extending his arm with it out of the cage.*

MONKEY-BOY: Go on, punk. You can have a piece. I won't bite you.

(HE *takes his arm back inside the bars as if his offer has been rejected, shrugs, and continues eating it.*)

Why don't you just get the hell out of here then, you little lot-louse? Go get me a left-handed monkey wrench, why don't you? Get me some light bulb grease. . . . Just get out of here.

(MONEY-BOY *sits at times and paces his cage at other times.*)

So you're the curious type, huh? Well, close your gaping pie hole before you catch flies. Came to see the freaks, huh? God, I hate those words "freaks" and "geeks." Huh? I ain't bitin' the heads off chickens or nothin'. I'm not a monster, okay? I don't have the curse of God on me. I'm a man, see.

(*Beat.*)

I like to think of myself as a hirsute individual. You know, special . . . and hairy. Now, my folks weren't hairy. My sister ain't hairy. . . . I, on the other hand, am hairy.

(*Beat.*)

So what's the big deal? I used to shave every day when I was your age. It took hours . . . and I was always cuttin' myself. Ma complained about the hair on the floor and Pa was always reachin' for the strap. I think they must have been ashamed of me. Me. . . their only son. That made me real sore, like I let them down or like a changeling had been left on their doorstep and they didn't know whether to raise it or bury it out back in an unmarked grave. So I split. I was about your age, I guess, 10, 11? Saw that little town, Eula, Oklahoma, in my rearview mirror and never looked back.

Now I'm big time, see? It wasn't always like this. I worked a little roughneck in the Louisiana oilfields, chopped cotton near Lafayette, washed cars in Waco. I seen the world . . . and it's overrated, kid. I been thrown out of more bars than there are on Beale Street. Been beat up more times than Max Baer and gotten paid a lot less, that's for sure. Hey, did you hear that Championship Heavyweight bout last month? You must have heard it. Zipperstein brought in the fight on this wireless set and we all sat around whoopin' and hollerin'. Baer put a whippin' on Schmeling. He was throwin' punches —

(MONKEY-BOY *shadowboxes in his cage.*)

— he was weavin' and duckin' in an' out —

(MONKEY-BOY *weaves and ducks while throwing punches.*)

— jabbin', settin' him up for the big one . . .

(MONKEY-BOY *jabs and then spins his whole body into a windmilling upper cut which* HE *delivers with such force that* HE *slips on the straw and falls on his rear.*)

(*Beat.* He *gets up and dusts* Himself *off.*)

Sorta like that, and the Kraut was down for the count. They say there were thirty thousand people screaming Max Baer's name in Yankee Stadium that night. The Hebe, our boss Al Zipperstein, was so happy our guy creamed that Nazi. Not that I ever seen a Nazi, but Al's pretty worked up about 'em, whatever they are.

(*Beat.*)

Where was I? Oh, yeah, the beatin's weren't the worst of the dirty jobs I had to take. No, the women were the worst, you know? Nah, you don't know about dames yet, do you? Well, take it from me they ain't all like your mama. You love your mama? Yeah, me too. I miss my mama. These dames, not your mama, are cute as hell. Curves all over and sometimes they smell sweet but inside they're hard as nails, they are. Good times and lots of kisses when you're flush, and goodbye, Charlie, when the dough runs out. Be careful of dames, kid, that's all I gotta say.

'Course this hair didn't help me any. They say when life hands out lemons make lemonade, but they never said nothin' about what to do when life hands you hair. Wanta feel it? (*Beat.*) That's okay, I don't blame you. Mostly the dames don't wanta feel it either. But now I'm on the upswing, see. Al tells everybody I'm the "Missing Link," whatever that is. And people are payin' good money to see me. It ain't Yankee Stadium yet but I hear them sayin' my name, "Monkey Boy, Monkey Boy." 'Course my name is really Billy, but they'll be cheerin' someday, you wait and see.

LETTERS FROM CUBA
BY MARIA IRENE FORNES

ENRIQUE *notices a picture of Fran on the wall.* HE *sits on a windowsill and begins talking to it.*

SCENE
New York

TIME
Today

ENRIQUE: Francisquita—

Do you remember when you came and brought us different kinds of food? Dry food, that was good once we soaked it in water, and food in cans. You apologized and said that food in cans was not as good as fresh food, but that you were not allowed to bring fresh food through customs. But it turned out that we loved food in cans. Mmmm.

At first you thought we were being polite to you because that was what you brought. But we really meant it. We liked food in cans. It had an American taste. A little taste of tin. When we ate it, we thought we were in the U.S. and spoke English to each other. We said, "Thank you"; "Water, please"; "How do you do?"; "Good morning"; "What is your name?"; "Do you speak Spanish?"

But also, it was good because we could use the cans as glasses to drink water, or pots to heat water for coffee or containers to put food in and save it in the refrigerator. We could make holes in the bottom and turn them into pots for plants. We grew beans, not too many, because the pots were small. And we also grew coffee. We kept one (without the holes) to put on the roof to collect water when it rains. Mother likes to wash her hair with rain water. I kept another in my room to hit with a spoon as a cowbell to use when I play music with my group. We also keep a candle in the sardine can. When the lights go out, Mama lights the candle. We thank you for the light.

When you came, we thought you might not like how we lost electric power so many times in one evening, and we told you we were sorry. You cheered us up and said, "Oh, no! Look how beautiful the light of the candle is when the room is dark." We looked, and we saw that you were right. We all looked elegant. You said, "This is how fancy restaurants are lit in New York, and Paris also." That did cheer us up and made us understand the irony of it. At home, we get depressed when we have to eat in the dark, and in rich places where they have electricity, they turn the lights off and light candles to make it look more elegant. So you see how much we have learned from you.

(ENRIQUE *goes over to Fran's picture and gives her a kiss.*)

LIGHT

BY JEAN-CLAUDE VAN ITALLIE

The love triangle of King Frederick the Great of Prussia, *a promiscuous scientist marquise, and the famous Voltaire carries them on a passionate, painful, incandescent voyage toward enlightenment and revolution.*

SCENE
Frederick, *a young prince here, in high boots, military trousers, and an open shirt, in prison, confides to the audience*

TIME
18th century

FREDERICK: (*To us.*) I'm 18, on maneuvers—staying in a barn. My father and his general are staying in another barn. We're close to the border. Tonight we're planning to escape. Katte—my equerry, my friend—Katte's arranged it all. I've had a red riding coat made. Hoof-beats in the courtyard. It's Katte. He's brought my horse. Clutching my new coat, I look out the window. It's not Katte. It's my father's general. We've been discovered! I drop the coat. I'm arrested, taken to the fortress of Kustrin and labeled "traitor." Four soldiers enter my cell. Am I about to be killed? An old general in the corner shakes his head sadly. "It's worse than that," he murmurs, pointing to the barred window. Terrified, I look out. Immediately I try to look away but there are hands around my head, like a vise. "The King's orders, Sir," says a giant grenadier. My father collects giant grenadiers, captures them all over Europe. I force myself to open my eyes. Surrounded by soldiers, my dear Katte, walking across the courtyard, waves almost merrily and blows me a kiss. He shouts, "Your Highness, forgive me!" I'm frozen. Katte, kneeling, places his head on the block. I don't see his head severed from his body—but I see it again and again. Katte, I kiss your eyes, your lips. For days I can't eat. Is it my turn next? The old general: "Be careful, Sir." And I am careful. I don't wish to die.

LOST LOVE

BY PETER PAPADOPOULOS

TITO, *a streetwise, Zenwise parking valet, is stranded on a mountaintop with Mitzy, a ditzy bride. Floodwaters have ripped through the wedding and all of the other guests and workers have disappeared in the sudden disaster. After Mitzy implies that she doesn't like valet parking,* TITO *tries to set the record straight.*

SCENE
The top of the world, biblical flooding below

TIME
The near future

TITO: (*Thick Hispanic accent.*)
What are you talking about?
Everybody likes valet parking.
It's like an extra special service
somebody parking your car
exceptional service
for the average man.
Or woman.
It's like
your special day
today

when someone is going to
pay this much attention to
your luxury
for the last few feet of your trip
and they're going to take special care
of your car
bring her around back
feed her some oats and water
brush down her coat
until it's silky smooth
while you relax
inside
comfortable
and very pleased
that you didn't have to get out of your car
in the *rain*
or the *wind*
or the *snow*
or the *sleet*
or the *hail*
or the *fog*
or the *freezing cold*
or the *smoggy heat*
and struggle across
the broiling hot pavement
sweat trickling down your armpits
your hair wilting, losing its shape
after all that work to make it look
just right—
and before you even get inside
for everybody to admire it.

VALET PARKING.
What's not to like?

LOST LOVE
BY PETER PAPADOPOULOS

Tito, *a streetwise, Zenwise parking valet, is stranded on a mountaintop with Mitzy, a ditzy bride, after floodwaters ripped through her wedding carrying away all the other guests and workers. Here,* Tito *calls on his years of therapy to convince a terrified Mitzy that even though* He *felt like killing her only moments ago —* He *won't, because many years of therapy and introspection have made* Him *a changed man.*

SCENE
A barren peak at the top of the world

TIME
The near future

Tito: (*Thick Hispanic accent.*):
    I have a bad temper.
    Sometimes I punch people.
    Not all the time.
    Just when they say something that hurts my feelings.
    That's what I learned in therapy.
    That I'm really quite sensitive.

(*Pause.*)

It's okay for a man to be sensitive, you know.
Violence is not the answer to everything.
Just because some people
are bothering you
harassing you,
calling you faggot
and shit
when you're not even gay,
well, just because they're calling me these names
it doesn't mean I should just crush them
use violence on them,
beat them,
shoot them,
crack their head with a baseball bat.
No, violence is not the answer.

There are other options available to an individual.
And sometimes
what seems like strength
is not really strength at all,
just a traditional way of
masking male insecurity.
Because it can often seem easier
to crush something
than to learn to coexist with it.
Because then you don't have to contend with
all of the difficulties that come with this . . .
trying relationship,
which can be
in fact

a hidden opportunity
for real growth.

Did you know that boys are more sensitive than girls?
If you take a baby away from its mother
on average
a baby boy will cry much faster than its female counterpart.
They're much more sensitive.

THE LUDICROUS TRIAL OF MR. P

BY SUSAN YANKOWITZ

This is the opening speech of the play. Defense Counsel LeMont *is a French man of any age between 30 and 70, quite huge in build and intellect.*

SCENE
Addressing the audience

TIME
1400s (but LeMont *is really a resident of any century!)*

LeMont: I take this opportunity for introduce myself, despite it is shame and *dommage* that educated people have ignorance of me. In my century, everyone — the whole world — know me by only the one name, same like your Madonna or Prince: LeMont! The mountain, is how you translate it. You never hear what I do to be the legendary *personage*? No? History do not begin when you born from womb, *mes amis*! You need lesson; I give you one. Medieval Europe and even up to twenty century, it happen often that domestic and wild animals prosecuted in court for crimes against man. Amazing, *oui*, but true. You look, you listen some little examples from court record.

(*Each of these sections should be spoken in the accent of the different countries.*)

Puglia, Italy, 1208. A wolf *mangia* the infant in his cradle and the court makes him lashed till skin breaks open and he exhibited in town square for *quatro* days as a warning to all the wolves who might see a little baby and think, "*Buon appetite!*"

County Clare, Ireland, 1470—and a dark day it was, a horse murdering a priest with three kicks to the head. The crowd dragged the beast to the hangman and in an hour the devil was swinging from a noose. But nooo! "Killing an animal in anger is not justice, it is revenge!" the judge proclaimed—and sent the hangman himself to the gallows!

Leipzig, Germany, 1843. A goat butt a child down a staircase into death. The jury sentence the goat to bury alive in mass grave with other criminals. What criminals? Who knows? How many? Maybe bulldozer counted.

Shanghai, China, 1885. Six wooden idols fall from ledge, crush life from high government officer. Heads of idols cut off, crowds cheering, and bodies thrown in pond for drowning.

Russia, 1591. When Prince Dmitri, son of Ivan II, was assassinated, the great bell of Uglich rang out the signal for revolution! Treason! So the bell put on trial and banished to coldest Siberia in company of eight *other* political prisoners.

(LeMont *now resumes speaking as himself.*)

You think I make up these stories? *Non, non.* Laws in Middle Ages say everything in universe, even insect, even flowerpot, must to be treated with dignity and *egalité,* same as human being, entitle to due process: defender, prosecutor, jury. How I know this? I am most famed defender of animals in world! My big case it happen in Provence, that is south France, 1421. The court call me — "LeMont! We entreat that you defend the rights for some poor creatures who cannot engage legal counsel for themselves." How can I refuse? I am busy man but *noblesse oblige*, I must sometimes give the pro bono. It is tremendous difficult job. My clients — you will be very amazement! — they are RATS who destroy the fields of barley and wheat and maybe make famine for the people, and also the TERMITES, a thousand, two thousand, maybe hundreds thousands! They have chewed up the foundation of Our Holy Lady Church and the cellars and walls are collapse! A crime *terrible*! Naturally they are indicted and must appear in court. And naturally they do not appear. I explain to Judge: "They mean no disrespect, Your Honor, but the rats, the termites, they live everywhere, in every smallest village. You will agree, I think, that a single summons could not reach them all?" He ponders and yes, it is so, he says — and orders that the summons be read the next Sunday from every pulpit in every parish in Provence!

C'est fou! C'est impossible for the suspects to appear, I tell him. "We must only to consider the length and difficulty of their journey from Aix or St. Remy to Avignon and the fatal perils along the way. The termites, how could they escape the ants below and the birds above who live only to make a dinner of them?! As for the rats — *mon Dieu!* — their mortal enemies, the cats, would be lying in wait for them at every corner and crossing! The journey, it would be suicide!"

This argument, it make the judge's head to spin — BUT he see that my logic have no holes. And the legal opinion make precedent — "If a criminal is ordered to make court appearance somewhere he cannot travel safely, he has lawful right to disobey for survival sake!" And this decision, it put hard cement on my international fame.

So justice demand the case versus the rats be dismissed. And justice for once prevail! St. Patrick, he rid his country of snakes. But LeMont, LeMont, he save from gruesome poisoning and extermination countless numbers of helpless creatures! I believe it is allowed to congratulate myself. The vermin, they do not spend one day in jail. . . .

But there are others, many others not so lucky to enjoy pursuit happiness. You must to look back, and then at the future where, I think, you are sitting now. You will see.

MAGGIE MAY

BY TOM O'BRIEN

CHARLIE *is a fisherman, and a self-proclaimed pleasure-seeker.*
HE *is trying to persuade Donny, with the help of some high-class marijuana, to stop being so cautious and to adopt his carefree lifestyle.*

SCENE
The docks of an island in the Bahamas

TIME
The present

CHARLIE: I mean, you're drinking Budweisers and smoking some cheap-ass, back-of-the-school-bus weed. It gets old. But if you drink the finest imported wines, have steak that melts in your mouth, scotch, cigars, this beautiful Jamaican herb — it is happiness. This is it. They don't want to tell you that. But here it is, my friend. Happiness. They don't know. The people writing the self-help books? The "happiness comes from within" bullshit? They don't got access to this stuff. How would they know happiness when they don't even know what the world has to offer? Do I look unhappy? Do I look like I'm searching for meaning in life? Like I'm looking for a soul mate to spend my golden years with? Fuck off! They're all golden years. I'm living a golden life. I beat the fucking system, kid.

[DONNY *is lost in his haze.*]

[CHARLIE: And then my grandpappy made love to me in an outhouse.

DONNY: What?

CHARLIE: Just seeing if you're still listening.

DONNY: Sorry.

CHARLIE: Thinking about your girl?

DONNY: No.

CHARLIE: Yeah, you are.

DONNY: Charlie, I'm not. I'm telling you.

CHARLIE: I been there, kid. I know what you're going through. Don't make decisions based on fear. That's death.

DONNY: I'm not. I . . .]

CHARLIE: Listen to me. Here's the deal, okay. There's all these lives out there just floating around waiting for you to live them. You have all these choices to make. Every choice you make splits things off into another parallel universe that's happening simultaneously to your own pathetic reality.

[DONNY: What?]

CHARLIE: There's two lives in front of you right this second. A fork in the road, shall we say. Two roads diverged in the yellow wood. Which one you gonna take, bubba, huh?

[DONNY: I don't know. Wait, what the fuck are you talking about?]

CHARLIE: Think about it. Most of the time we're too afraid to live. We say, "I couldn't do that. I couldn't be with her. I don't want to be happy." We talk ourselves out of living. But it's still out there. It's waiting for you. It's happening whether you choose it or not. It's just a question of whether you're gonna go for the ride or sit on the sidelines hopin' and dreamin'. All you have to do is step into it. (*Beat.*) A life unlived is not a life at all.

THE MEAN REDS

BY MARK SCHARF

After seeing his alcoholic wife through recovery, MIKE *then suffers a bitter divorce from her.* HE *is talking to two friends who have dropped by to see how* HE *is doing on his birthday.*

SCENE
MIKE DRENNON's *house on the outskirts of a small town on Maryland's Eastern Shore*

TIME
The present

MIKE: The only good thing about this birthday is that I don't have to put up with my in-laws. Hell, now that I think about it, my life won't be infected by those people at all. I won't miss my drunken, whining fruitcake soon-to-be-ex mother-in-law who passed her neurotic genes down to my soon-to-be-ex wife. And I sure won't miss Rose's nasty, fat, manipulative bitch of a sister and her foul family either. Every time they come over here I have to lock myself in the bathroom so I won't kill one of them. They think I have a weak bladder. I just can't stand to be in the same house with them for more than ten minutes. You met them. How could you forget? That doofus-looking moron of a husband with a voice like a demented cartoon, "Uhhh, how're you doin', Sport?" The guy is bald straight up the middle, so he grows these three hairs from the side of his head out about four feet long and he curls them all together across his bald spot in a spiral pattern and shellacs them down on his head with about four cans of hair spray. His bald spot is all shiny from the hair spray and it shines through these huge pinwheels of stiff hair. He's about six foot four and he's spastic — he walks into the house and BAM! "Ohhhh, I'm sorry! Did I do that? Yuck, yuck, yuck."

Yeah, they're charming all right. Rose's sister is about three feet shorter than her husband and about three feet wider. All she cares about is money and looking down her nose at everybody else. She thinks her children are these perfect, beautiful angels when she's got them as screwed up as she is. They gave me the flu last winter. The nasty little mucous machines are always sick. They're like little walking petri dishes of disease who get my kids sick every single time they come over here. And they look like a combination of the worst features of their parents. The boy looks like Moe of the Three Stooges and is about as bright. The girl's a nasty butterball with a face like Alfred E. Neuman on the cover of a *Mad* magazine. They're not children. They're evil infectious trolls. I could never eat a piece of my own birthday cake 'cause I had to let one of them help me blow out the candles and they'd spit all over the cake. And at least one of them would find a way to sneeze on it.

Hate can be a very good thing, Mary Jo. There are some things that you should hate, that you need to hate like Nazis, and cancer — and my wife and her nasty family. A nice, healthy hate.

MEASURE FOR PLEASURE: A RESTORATION ROMP

BY DAVID GRIMM

As valet to a British lord, WILL BLUNT *is the classic clown figure found in Restoration comedy. Here,* HE *contemplates the meaning of happiness while resisting a bottle of gin, or trying to.* BLUNT *is discovered, with his playing cards. An unopened bottle of gin before him.* HE *reaches for the bottle and stops himself.*

SCENE
The Lustforth home, below stairs

TIME
1751, during the forty days known in the Christian calendar as Lent, which ends with the Spring Solstice

BLUNT: No. No, I mustn't. Mustn't mustn't mustn't. Pick a card, any card. I'll tell you what you got. The Queen of Misery, that's what. Who was the stupid pillock first thought love brings happiness? Love is scenes and screams and jealousy and acting like a cunt. I'll tell you a secret: No one has the first idea what makes 'em truly happy. "If only I was rich and tall and had a smaller bum." "If I had nicer clothes and whiter teeth and people laughed at all my jokes and wanted to have sex with me." If only if only if only. No. Seamus — that's the only bloke I ever knew was truly happy. Dear wee Seamus down the pub who, standing up, was all of four foot eight. Used to be a chimney sweep. Not much job fulfillment covered in soot, coughing up black phlegm and — to add insult to injury — one day he fell in love. Yeh. Down the lane and round the bend there lived the Widow Thwacker. Big as a bloody Amazon, she was. Breasts like cannons and a face out of the Book of Revelations. Tortured him, she did. I tell you, it was nothing short of torture. And Seamus moping, pining, cursing his fate: criminal. Finally, poor bleeder couldn't take it anymore. Got properly pissed as a Dutchman and, with a fist packed full o' daisies, he comes knocking at her door. She thinks he's havin' her on, so she cuffs him twice about the head and slams the door shut on his hand. Now, friends, a sensible bloke might, when faced with this, give up. But not our Seamus. No. Each Sunday for three months he comes and stands there at her door. And each Sunday for three months, she growls and hits him on the head. "Why do you mock me, chimney sweep?" she says to him at last. Know what he says? "I do not mock you, beauty. You are the goddess of my dreams, my every waking hope's desire. You are truth made flesh and bliss incarnate. Widow Thwacker, I'm in love." I mean, for God's sake! And that's not the end of it, 'cos then and there he kisses her! On the lips! (Though considering his height, it may not have been the ones on her face.) And what did he feel at that moment? Pleasure? Arousal? Happiness? I'll tell you what he felt, he felt the marble bust of *Mister* Thwacker come crashing down on his head. And she brought it down with such enormous force that his wee brain became unstuck and rattled round inside his skull. Now he still sits at his same corner down the local pub, but oh the grin he shines is one the like of which you've never seen. 'Course, he drools into his beer and wets himself when he forgets to go, but the Widow Thwacker's there beside him tending him with care, for (as she likes to say), "This Seamus is the happiest little bugger I have known." So I ask you, is that what a man must do to find his bliss? Is happiness only for children and the mentally deranged? Perhaps that is the price we pay to learn to be adults. What's an adult then but a sad and lonely git who doesn't have the merest clue of how to see or think or feel or talk to anyone at all. If happiness is born of innocence, I want it back. I want to run and laugh and dance and know that I'm alive. But more than that I want to know how to make Molly happy. I want to be the one who can. I want it to be me. So go on then: Pick a card. Any card. It won't make a sodding difference. Happiness—Hell, I'll drink to that. (BLUNT *grabs up the bottle of gin, opens it and swigs.*)

THE MERCY SEAT

BY NEIL LABUTE

On his way to work at the World Trade Center on September 11, 2001, BEN *stopped off to see Abby, his lover and boss, and thus escaped the catastrophe. A married man with children,* BEN *has been reluctant to inform his wife of his whereabouts. Instead,* HE *now feels that* HE*'s been presented a golden opportunity to erase the past and start a new life with Abby.*

SCENE
A spacious New York apartment

TIME
September 12, 2001

BEN: Right? I mean, Jesus . . . you think I was born this way, like some cutthroat *pirate* of the high seas? Huh? Hell, I'm just trying to muddle through, that's all, just muddle my fucking way through to middle age, see if I can make it that far. You like trivia so goddamn much, well, here's a little tidbit for ya . . . I'm *faking* it. Okay? Totally getting by on fumes. I put my game face on and go out there and I'm scared shitless. (*Beat.*) You know what? I take that back. . . . This *is* me. I've screwed up every step of my life, Abby, I'm not afraid to admit it. Happy to, actually, I am happy to sing it out there for anybody who wants to hear. I always take the easy route, do it faster, simpler, you know, whatever it takes to get it done, be liked, get by. That's me. Cheated in school, screwed over my friends, took whatever I could get from whomever I could take it from. My marriage, there's a goddamn fiasco, of which you're intimately aware. The kids . . . I barely register as a dad, I'm sure, but compared to the other shit in my life, I'm Doctor-fucking-*Spock*. No matter what I do or have done, they adore the hell out of me, and I'm totally knocked out by that. What kids are like. Yeah. (*Beat.*) And you, let's not forget you. *Us*. Okay, yes, I haven't done all that I've promised, said I'd do, I fuck up along the way. All right. But I'm trying, this time out—with you, I mean—I have been trying. Don't know what it looks like, feels to you, but I have made a real go of us, and that is not a lie. It isn't. And so then, yesterday . . . through all the smoke and fear and just, I dunno, *apocalyptic* shit . . . I see a way for us to go for it, to totally erase the past—and I don't think it makes me Lucifer or a criminal or some bad man because I noticed it. I really don't. We've been given something here. A chance to . . . I don't know what, to wash away a lot of the, just, rotten crap we've done. More than anything else, that's what this is. A chance. I know it is.

MY CHEKHOV LIGHT
BY FRANK GAGLIANO

A theatre professor nearing or just past 60, PETER PARADISE *stands on a scaffold arranging lights in a college theatre while conversing with Martin Starr, a former beloved student who has made it big in television by selling out his craft.* PETER *refuses to let Martin or Carl, his student lighting assistant, into the theatre; they are unseen and unheard, but can hear* PETER.

SCENE
Bodoni County Junior College

TIME
The present

PETER PARADISE: What?! — "Bitter?" Moi? " — Insulting?" Wherever did you get that?

— Of course I'm bitter! Of course I'm insulting! I had dreams for you, Martin; hopes for you, Martin. You were one of those rare student actors with talent and brains! And I knew you were going to make it and you knew you were going to make it and when you made it — you *said* — you'd pump the "obscene TV bucks" — your phrase, not mine — back into a theatre of substance and language and startling visions; into what I used to call—and in a phrase you would love to hear—what I used to call "the entertainment that confronts"; and you also said—No! Promised!—that you would keep your stage talent sharp, even while making your "obscene TV bucks"; and I believed you! because I needed to believe you, because *I* had stopped making "entertainment that confronts" and so—and, oh, how I do understand the five-and-dime psychology of it all—I needed to believe it from the person I was living through; the son, perhaps? I was depending on, perhaps? to fill out what once had been my vision? Perhaps.

Because I could feel that whatever vision—not to mention "energy"—I still had,

was going,

kept going,

had gone.

But you did not keep your talent sharp, and you held on to your "obscene TV bucks"—until now! And I know why you've come back to Bodoni County, Martin Starr, né Starovich—to your alma mater, Martin Starr, né Starovich. You're here, Martin, to talk about giving the school a large check—a very large check, I'm told, to build a new theatre here—to tear down this space—this very space we're in—my space—my space where we've been programming my Chekhov-Kaleidoscope—tear it down to build a new space, a new theatre—to be called—what?—The Martin Starr Theatre?—Oh! Cheap shot?! You don't have that kind of an ego? Hm. We'll see. And if I'm wrong I'll apologize. But understand! I don't want you to give your obscene bucks to this institution! So that my space can be torn down—and I intend to stop you!!!

NO! don't come down "to calm me down"—not in here, I said!—the door!—Don't open!—the light! THE LIGHT! Blinding! I'll slip!—back in!—get back up there!

. . . yes. better. keep eyes closed. just for a second.

. . . yes.

Now I'm coming down!

—No! Stay in there! Stay up there!—I'll MANAGE ALONE!

. . . There.

You see? I'm do

ing fine.

I'm com

ing down fine.

I can do it with

out your help—

with

out

any

one's

help.

—NO, CARL! YOU, TOO! YOU STAY UP THERE!

There.

Feet on

the stage—on my stage!

. . . Good.

'NAMI
BY CHAD BECKIM

ROACHIE, *a Black/Latino in his late 20s, has come home late after spending the day smoking crack and gambling with the rent money. Here HE lies about these activities to his wife, Keesha.*

SCENE
A shoebox apartment in Corona, Queens, New York City

TIME
Late evening

ROACHIE: I woulda been heah like on time, cept I couldn't stop lookin at tha moon. Yo, you shoulda seen it, baby. That shit was fuckin amazin! I was walkin towards tha buildin an juss looked up and, boom! It was so ill. I had ta go up ta tha roof ta look at it. It was like, like tha kinda moon you see in them movies bout California or tha Wild West? Juss fuckin huge an orange an so, so bright! An I'm sittin there, all like, hypnotized an shit, juss starin at it. An I started thinkin of you—funniest shit, me lookin at tha moon an thinkin of you, knowin you prolly waitin for me in tha apartment, prolly heated at me—but I couldn't make myself leave. An then, like, boom, I remembered—tha only other time I evah seen tha moon look like that was tha night when we was at that club in Ozone? Member? Like, one of tha first times we evah went out-out, like on a date out? An that Dominican niggah came out his face at you, an I gave that niggah tha beat-down of his life for disrespectin you, an afterwards we was sittin on some park bench, lookin at tha moon an talking? You member that night? How tha moon was? I was up there, on tha roof, lookin at tha moon an thinkin of you, thinking how I should get you ta see it, an then, before I knew it, it like, went away or whutevah. Got all, normal an shit. I'm sorry you ain't see it, baby. That shit was hot. So thass where I been. (*Beat.*) Whah? Whah you lookin at me like that for?

THE NATURALIST
BY ROBIN GOLDFIN

This monologue was inspired by a letter in a British birding magazine. One actor, age 20s to 50s, can portray both THE NATURALIST *and* THE YOUNG SCOUT. HE *should experiment and enjoy playing with the range of ages and accents.*

SCENE
A small town in the north of England. THE NATURALIST *is speaking to an audience at an Annual Scouting Awards dinner.*

TIME
Just last year

> (*Lights up on an actor in hiking gear and a suitable helmet.* HE *is in the middle of his speech and has a strong north of England accent.*)

THE NATURALIST: . . . Sole access to the attic was via trap door in the ceiling. By precarious means—I realize now how soon I might have departed this life—I entered the loft and recorded egg laying, hatching, and fledging. For my tree, I chose the flowering cherry in the garden, recording bud changes, first leaves, first flowers, first fruits, and their development. My school was Highly Commended, and two medals were awarded, one to me.

So began my love affair with Nature. It is impossible to estimate the influence of these early events on my development . . . as today I stand before you not to accept yet another award, but to pass on the legacy . . . of love. I know we are all waiting impatiently to hear from this year's winner, who has so diligently devoted him/her self to observing these creatures in their native surroundings! So—without further ado: The Tree Warden Society of The Home Parish Council of Wombourne, South Staffordshire, hereby presents a FIRST for Animal in Its Natural Habitat Appreciation to—

Scout Ernesto Hermon and his outstanding work, "Defenestration and the Little Finches."

Ernesto, do come up and tell us—how does it feel to come first?

(*Lights up on the audience. The actor on stage quickly discards the helmet and part of his gear to reveal scouting attire as* HE *becomes* THE YOUNG SCOUT, ERNESTO. HE *should distinguish* THE YOUNG SCOUT *by both age and accent. Perhaps a Cockney?* HE *begins shyly.*)

This is my first time. I don't know what to say. There are so many people I—I couldn't have done this without me Mum, me Da, the good Lor—

(*Suddenly* HE *sees something and freezes. Cautiously* HE *gropes in his pocket for a telescope and slowly extends it—the sexual metaphor should not be lost—*HE *can barely contain his excitement.*)

Don't move. Don't breathe. . . . (*Scanning the audience.*) There! A snag-toothed warbling frustration! And there—a belly-throated regret! Wait, it couldn't be—it is! A red-breasted lust! And right next to her—the sleek-throated shame! Oh, what a pair . . . this is my. . . . Ah!. . . The full-breasted loneliness is feeding her babies! Oh! The flat-footed failure is laying an egg!. . . (*Gasp!*) — I don't believe — so rarely seen in these parts: A dark-hued blue-crested sadness. (*Whistles.*) Look at that wing span . . .

(HE *exits looking through the telescope.*)

NEW YORK
BY DAVID RIMMER

THE CAREGIVER *can be virtually any age—*HE *just needs to show the strain of his profession, dealing with a phenomenal number of patients. The scene was written as part of a full-length play commissioned for a benefit for 9/11 victims, so on one level it can be taken as a man living through the aftermath of that time, which was an overwhelming period for therapists. On another level it could just be a universal expression of stress, overwork, and personal pain, all mixed up with a crazy sense of humor.*

SCENE
A psychiatrist's office

TIME
Fall 2001

CAREGIVER: So I get to the office. There's a manic depressive, two paranoid schizophrenics, a delusional, a denial, a psychotic episode, two unresolved Oedipal complexes, father and son—an anal retentive, an anal explosive, an anal compulsive, an anal confused. Post-traumatic stress disorder—big on that now. A little syndrome, a little deficit, a little this, a little that. Just another day at the orifice.

Dreams, fantasies—low self-esteem, high penis envy, fear of phobia. Obsessive-compulsive disorder, compulsive-obsessive disorder, rejection, projection, protection, detection, confection, which direction? "Help! I need help! Help!" So do I! Jeez! D'you have any idea?

Nightmares, hallucinations, fear of interpersonal relationships, a partridge in a pear tree. A guy who keeps asking, "Do babies get boners? Do babies get boners?" The acid flashback that never ends—takes a lickin' and keeps on tickin'! Triskadeskaphobia—fear of Triscuits. The screaming meemees—Nature-Nurture! Nurture-Nature! Yin yang, walla walla bing bang!—Yes, babies get boners!. . .

I have that dream where you go back to college and you don't know the course and you take the final exam? Except I go back to med school. I know the course, I ace the final exam, I take everybody in the class's final exam, I take everybody in the school's final exam, I go before all the teachers' review boards and I ace them—and I end up ruling the world but I have to abdicate because of insomnia. If I could get some sleep, I could have that other dream that I like so much, the one where the ham sandwich eats me. Jeez, who do you go to when you get burned out? And who does he go to? And him and him and him and her and her and her, all the way down to the last guy—and who does he go to? Me?. . . Cause that's scary. I haven't messed up my job . . . yet. I'm fine, aren't I? I'm fine. You know what I need? More patients. You know any? I had a girlfriend somewhere along the line. Infantile sexuality. God, I'd kill for some infantile sexuality now.

(*Sad and tired.*)

Grief. Despair. Loss. Loneliness. Fear. Anxiety. The shakes. Just an old-fashioned case of the blues. Whatever you call it, they got it. Tommy, Jenny, Rashid, Miguel, Heather, Dov, Angie, Guiseppe, Bob, Fred, Tasha, Kelly, Mr. Winters.

(*Takes a breath.*)

And that was Tuesday. Before lunch.

ON MY HEAD

BY THADDEUS RUTKOWSKI

THE SPEAKER *is a 30-something Asian-American man whose native language is English.* HE *has dark, straight, medium-length hair.* HE *is dressed casually: jeans, dark sneakers, a solid-color shirt.*

SCENE
Anywhere, USA

TIME
The present

SPEAKER: My first haircut was a flattop. I got it below street level, in a decrepit barbershop my father took me to. Outside, there was a kinetic red-and-white signpost. Inside, there were cast-iron chairs with leather strops hanging from their sides. The whole place smelled like scalps.

The barber used electric clippers on my head. Behind my ears, the clippers made my entire skull vibrate. Then the barber applied a paste that made my head look like a burr.

I used a comb on my head, along with a large dose of goop. When I was finished, my head looked like a skillet.

Later, my mother gave me a trim. When she was finished, I looked like I was wearing a helmet that had failed to stop a grazing bullet.

For a long while I stayed away from barbers of all stripes. My hair grew until it reached my back.

One day I saw some boys with Mohawk cuts. But these boys weren't Mohawks; they weren't even Native Americans. They were just a couple of white boys trying to look like Native Americans. Even so, I decided to get a brush of my own.

One night I went into a convenience store, and the cashier asked me, "What are you?"

"I'm a boy," I said, "I guess."

"Seriously," the cashier said, "I can't tell."

Another time, at a border between countries, a guard looked at my passport and asked, "Who is this? Is this a little girl?"

"It is not time for jokes," I said in the guard's language.

"For me," the guard said in my language, "it is always time for jokes."

On another occasion I walked through an airport and was stopped by two plainclothesmen. "Do you take acid?" they asked. "You look like you do."

Later, a girlfriend talked me into getting a layered style and a body wave. After I got them, she said, "You look so good I want to have sex with you right now."

Later still, I was invited to a "clipping party," where men with short hair were getting their hair cut even shorter by a barber wearing Army fatigues. The sergeant/barber buzzed the clip-ees' heads with electric shears. A man with a razor hanging from his belt stood nearby. He said his name was Bic. I flipped through a scrapbook of boot-camp photographs, but I didn't sign up for a haircut.

One time, I met a performer whose hair was shaped like a cylinder. The cylinder was about twelve inches high. I spoke to him, but our conversation had nothing to do with appearance. The next time we met, the cylinder was gone and he was wearing a hair net.

These days I go to a cutter who has hair that resembles my own. When he asks me what I want, I say, "I want my hair short in places but long in others. I want it long enough for a ponytail, but I also want to see bare scalp. I want words scored in the stubble. I want to wear ceremonial hair gear. I want to be stopped by cops. I want to be on television. I want groupies. I want a style among the top one hundred. I want to meet relatives. I want to be photographed with family."

ORSON'S SHADOW

BY AUSTIN PENDLETON

KENNETH TYNAN, *a British drama critic, early 30s with a smoker's cough, has suggested that Orson Welles direct Laurence Olivier in Ionesco's* Rhinoceros. *Welles and Olivier are about to arrive for the first reading. The stage manager has just gone off into the wings.*

SCENE
The stage of the Gaiety Theatre in Dublin. There is a ghost light. Furniture of a medieval tavern is scattered across the stage.

TIME
1960

KEN: (HE *indicates us, moves forward and addresses us.*) I didn't want to turn that nice young man into a receptacle for exposition. However willing he might be. I mean, this could have turned into one of those dreadful scenes in which he asks me questions and I answer them, until, with clumsy spontaneity, we have told the audience the entire forty-five years of Orson's life to date. Like the maid who answers the telephone at the beginning of the play. (HE *mimes a phone and imitates a maid.*) "Hello? Oh, I'm sorry, Mr. Welles has stepped out—well, you see, he's walking on the moors—well, I don't know how long, you see he's brooding—Why is he brooding?—Because they tore up 'is contract at RKO in 1941 — How many years ago was that? — Well, nineteen years, wasn't it, because you know what year it is now — You don't? — It's 1960! — Oh, it's been nineteen long and bitter years 'ere, yes, they tore up that contract after 'e made *Citizen Kane*, took away 'is right to final cut they did, and 'im having lost his mum to the jaundice when he was nine, poor little tyke — What's final cut? — Well, Mr. Zanuck, final cut is where nobody can touch the filum after Mr. Welles cuts it the way 'e likes it, and they took it away after *Citizen Kane*, they did — What's *Citizen Kane*? Why just today the gardener says to me, 'Bessie, it revolutionized the art of the motion picture! I particularly admire his use of deep focus.'" (*Back to his own voice.*) Well, you see what I mean. The plays were like that. Oh, I fought it. With every breath in my body, which is not saying a great deal because I really do smoke too much, but of course no one took really seriously a word I wrote. You see, I am a critic. What is a critic? A critic is no one. A critic is a man who cowers in a train compartment before a woman whose baleful eyes are saying, "I'm sure I have no idea why you were so unkind to poor Vivien Leigh." I tell you, I came to cherish the idea that there was more to life than this. And so I decided to approach Sir Laurence Olivier — my hero, really, in case you're interested — to ask if I might work with him to create the National Theatre of Great Britain, which he is soon to form, to, well, advise him. I realized that if I'm to get him to hire me I must present him with an idea that will appall him so much he will always remember it was not his. Well, he needs a director for a play he's doing, and I'm proposing Orson. I'm using Orson. I'm using my best friend. I'm using the man I wish had been my father. My real father was not, you see, married to my mother. I am illegitimate. This is an advantage for a critic, actually, as when you write harshly of someone and they call you a bastard, you can receive it as a simple statement of fact. What is the point of what I'm saying? Oh, yes. No, I'm not using Orson, I am trying to help him. All those films he made since *Citizen Kane*, since they took away his right to final cut, all those marvelous films butchered by the studios, I feel grief, raw grief when I think about it, mitigated only slightly by the fact that it was his own fucking fault. Or much of it. Or not much of it at all, really. I don't know. Do you have friends like this? Never mind.

ORSON'S SHADOW

BY AUSTIN PENDLETON

At the suggestion of the British drama critic KENNETH TYNAN, *Orson Welles is directing Laurence Olivier in Ionesco's* Rhinoceros. *Rehearsals have begun and Orson no longer feels welcome on the project.* KEN *and Orson are onstage, tense and silent. After a moment,* KEN *comes forward and speaks to us.*

SCENE
The stage of the Royal Court Theatre in London. Perhaps part of the set for Rhinoceros *is in place.*

TIME
1960

KEN: We're two weeks in. It's been — it's been — I must say I've been harsh sometimes about things I have reviewed. Particularly if it's been the work of people I admire. I suppose I've thought if they're capable of greatness they should bloody well achieve it! That surely all they need is a cheerfully administered humiliation, as by a brisk, demented, fourth-form rugby coach, to lash them on. What I see now is that they've done anything of any worth at all is a miraculous achievement. Because they are in fact insane. [(*Orson gets up, leaves the stage.*)] He hates it when I talk like this. But then I talk too much when I'm around him. I've followed him for years all over Europe like a yapping hound pursuing a large, drifting air balloon, as he floated about, after his exile from Hollywood in 1948, trying to raise money for his films himself, from Hungarians and Middle Easterners, at long dinners in hotel dining rooms in Venice and Madrid, in which he told them of his dreams of filming *Don Quixote* or of finishing his filming of *Othello*, and they asked him what it was like to have sex with Rita Hayworth. Or, if they mentioned his work at all, why he hadn't made a decent film since *Citizen Kane*. And he believes that that's what I think, too, which it is not. I try to tell him he's a living genius, and once one is called a living genius one only exists to disappoint. I tell him the only reason that they miss those early works is that they want to be that age again, discovering him, discovering the world, but, wait, I tell him, when he's dead they'll see the value of everything he's done —

O. T. FAIRCLOUGH AND ROGER MAIS

BY CLIFFORD MASON

ROGER MAIS, *a social revolutionary and prolific writer from Jamaica, explains to legendary editor O. T. Fairclough that the aftermath of independence from white colonial rule is not going to be easy or equitable for all Jamaicans.*

SCENE
Jamaica, during a dockworkers' strike

TIME
1940

ROGER MAIS: When independence comes you will have a complete and clear majority. Means you can do anything you want, anything. But it'll take a while. First you'll have to train the yard boys, the brethren, the rank and file how to read and write and ride in an elevator and wear shoes every day and how to eat with a knife and fork. I know, just outside this office there are a dozen people who can read and write and know how to ride in an elevator and how to eat with a knife and fork. And they'll all be wearing shoes. But that's because they'll all be the middle class, whatever their color. They went to the right college, have the right family name, live in the right neighborhood. But they're less than one percent of all Jamaicans. Now if we were in the country or the ghetto I doubt if you'd find one in thirty who could pass on all points. Don't get me wrong, feet work better without shoes as long as they don't have to walk on hard man-made surfaces, and eating with your hands is the most civilized way to eat. As to reading and writing, well, the thirst for knowledge is certainly there. Go down into town and you'll see a man at the top of King Street, in the yard next to the parish church, reading the newspaper out loud to at least two dozen people. As for the elevator. Well, technology can intimidate the most sophisticated of us. A president of the United States, William Henry Harrison, was the first resident of the White House after the electric light was installed, and he was so afraid of it he wouldn't go near it, not even to turn it on or off. The black servants had to do it. Each morning they would arrive for work and find all the lights in the White House burning from the night before. Only then were they turned off. So what is the point? Just this. You'll never have the idyll of independence that you're dreaming of, even after the Englishman leaves and your ninety-nine percent try to take over. Because by then it will be too late. The black middle class, the jet black ones, are the worst snobs, the worst racists, the most cruel of all masters and the most abject of black Englishmen. And you damn well know it. You think after worshipping Lord Haw-Haw's fourteenth class of Englishman for three hundred years they're going to throw out the caste system, get rid of domestic service, do away with graft for every petty bureaucratic service that's theirs by right anyhow, respect a black face that isn't educated and well off just because it's a black face and what they've come from. If you do you're a bigger fool than I take you for. I can go anywhere on this island, anywhere, good neighborhood or bad, and I'll be treated like a king because of my half-white face. The ones who hate me know they can't do a damned thing about it because there's too much power behind that half-white face. And when the day comes that they can kill me and get away with it, it'll be too late. The only thing they'll want to kill for then is power, raw naked power. And they'll kill you as soon as kill me if that's how they can get it. And they'll be right because you don't represent them, you represent yourself. You even represent me. And no matter how much you despise the black middle class, you're one of them. Would you let your daughter marry a servant's son? Hell no. And that's what's going to destroy your idyll. By the time the Englishman leaves it will be too late. He'll have corrupted you beyond the point of redemption. He probably already has.

THE PARIS LETTER

BY JON ROBIN BAITZ

Although Sandy has been married to Katie for some twenty years, he remained friends with ANTON, *his ex-lover, until Burt came on the scene, and Sandy fell for him.*

SCENE
An empty stage

TIME
February 2001

ANTON: Yes. Once he was married, all of Sandy's raging internal wars had been more or less won. It seemed.

Yes. It was in the 1980s that he relaxed. Happiness deepened and sharpened his instincts for the work he did. Katie became well known, beloved in New York, writing two terrific cookbooks and giving sold-out, highly coveted classes at the restaurant.

And their home! A gorgeous white living room, comfortable, piled high with books and flooded with light! It was one of those places you just want to be in, and I spent a lot of time there. With

Sandy, Katie, and Sam, my magnificent godson, who grew into a wise, clever, funny and bold boy, adored by his mother and cherished by his stepfather.

And then Burt happened.

I don't want to bore you with facts, as they were exhaustively reported for the benefit of all. The press gloated over, and endlessly explored, the thrilling "circumstances" surrounding Burt Sarris and his rather predictable, Icarus-like fall. And suicide. They made fun of the young movie stars, rock stars, and Hollywood agents who lost fortunes to Burt. Poor Burty. He attempted to stanch the flow from the upper reaches of his clientele with money from the quote "non-famous, non-celebrities" . . . who collapsed. Rather like dominos. Bang. Bang. Bang. (He *takes a deep breath and gets his bearings.*) In November of the new century's first year . . . down go the Meyersons, the Bermans, the Golds, the Orrs—these ex-clients of Sandy were now dispossessed—stripped of privilege—wandering in the new American fiscal diaspora, like all the other poor schmucks—wondering where their good luck had gone. . . . (*Beat.*) Yes. There is no more money. Sandy's personal fortune of seventy-five million dollars to stanch the flow, gone! The house on West Tenth Street, gone. The few remaining pieces of art and a tiny island in Maine, all gone . . . the creditors took it all. (*Beat. Sigh. The lights are changing slowly.*) Right. It is February 2001, the night my story began. . . . Remember? It is very late, or very early in the morning, 2 AM. Sandy has just left Burt's, yes, just left Burt's, unaware that Burt has taken his advice and killed himself. Earlier that day, there had been a spate of wild phone action, followed by frantic meetings with the vengeful lawyers of the panicked ex-clients of Sandy, who felt as if they had been handed over to Burt Sarris very much like lambs to the slaughter.

THE PAVILION
BY CRAIG WRIGHT

At their twentieth high school reunion, classmates (played mostly by the male NARRATOR) reminisce about and/or mourn old times. In this speech, the male NARRATOR becomes LISA, who organized the festivities.

SCENE
The Pavilion, an old dance hall in the fictional town of Pine City, Minnesota

TIME
The present

NARRATOR: It's eight thirty-two. The dinner dishes have been cleared away by the teenagers in their black pants and white shirts, thirty-five dollars for one night of work. And there's a woman standing on the stage, talking into a microphone that obviously isn't working, and then suddenly, with a pop and a squeal, it is.

(*The* NARRATOR *becomes* LISA. *Note: the year of the graduating class can be moved forward to reflect the change in production date.*)

NARRATOR: (*As* LISA, *to audience.*) Is everybody having a good time? Fabulous! For those of you who don't know me, I'm Lisa

Gulbranson, and I know you've all been here for a while, having a wonderful dinner and catching up with each other, but now let me formally welcome you, on behalf of the whole reunion committee, (which is essentially me and Angie), to the Class of 1985's Twentieth Reunion! Yay! There's some school spirit! Pine City Panthers, P-C-P! I see a lot of familiar faces out there! And don't everybody forget we've got Skippy Schouviller from Ingebretsen Photography set up right over there all night taking pictures, so if you want your picture taken with the *old gang*, you just talk to him.

Now, when we first started planning this party, Angie and I thought it would be fabulous if we could get The Mustangs back together to play. But it didn't take long for us to realize only two of the original Mustangs were still with us: Eddie Gieselhardt and Peter Mollberg. Then we never got an RSVP from Peter . . . naughty. But, even *worse*, last month, as many of you probably have heard, Eddie was killed in a car accident on his way to a gig in Fargo. So when Peter called and told us last week he'd be coming, I asked him if he could just play us all a song, to remember and whatever, in Eddie's honor. So, before we head into the dancing portion of the evening, let me introduce to you, and it makes me kinda sad to say this, the Class of 1985's Vice-President, and the only surviving member of The Mustangs, Peter Mollberg!

THE PAVILION
BY CRAIG WRIGHT

PETER MOLLBERG *returns to his twentieth high-school reunion to confront his guilt over deserting his pregnant girlfriend, Kari, after their senior year.* HE *confesses to an old classmate, now a minister, that he's never been able to get past that terrible mistake.*

SCENE
The Pavilion, an old dance hall in the fictional town of Pine City, Minnesota

TIME
The present

PETER: It's like . . .

[NARR: (*Bored.*) What?]

PETER: No, you don't want to hear about this.

[NARR: (*Relieved.*) OK.]

PETER: It's like when I said No to Kari back then, when I left town?

[NARR: (*Slightly impatient.*) Yeah?]

PETER: It's like I got on the wrong train, you know? And I've been on this train now for twenty years, and Jesus, I don't want to go where this train is going, I really don't.

[NARR: Where do you want to go?]

PETER: I want to go . . . I want to go where I maybe could have gone with her, you know?. . . if I had been more . . . I don't know, strong or something. When I saw Kari for the first time, Smoke, I'll never forget it; it was like the first or second week of high school and I walked into the audiovisual lab and there she was. And I swear—I couldn't have put this into words back then, but it's all I think about lately—it was really like I recognized her or something. And I don't mean it like we'd met before or anything. We'd never met. It was just—it was as if in her face—in her beauty—I was finally seeing the beauty of everything, you know?. . . the unreachable beauty of the whole world that I'd always felt inside and tried to hold onto but never could, it was all in her. The whole universe had articulated itself in her. To me. That's just how I saw it. And I just knew that if I could be with her—by her side, you know?—then I could be alive and be part of things. I'd at least have a chance. Now I know it sounds crazy, Smoke, I know, given everything that's happened, and there's a lot of water gone under the bridge, and a lot of time has passed, and there's been a lot of stupid shit and I've done most of it, but when I see her now, I still feel the same way. I look at her and I still see it, I see her face and I think, "Oh, there you are—the world. Where have you been?" I love her, you know? I screwed up back then, there's no getting around it, but I love her. I think she's great. I love her.

[NARR: Have you told her that?

PETER: No.

NARR: Don't.]

A PICASSO

BY JEFFREY HATCHER

Under interrogation by a German art critic, PABLO PICASSO *is asked to authenticate an early drawing so the Nazis can burn an original Picasso. On the eve of his sixtieth birthday,* HE *relates the following account of the painting's origin, to either enlighten or mislead the interrogator, Miss Fischer.*

SCENE
A vault below the streets of Paris

TIME
After lunch on a late October day, 1941

PICASSO: (*Interrupts.*) I was never "little"! I was the firstborn. And I was born dead. No breath. The family wailed to see my face, so blue. My first memory is the sound of crying. My mother, my grandmother, aunts. Like a funeral. When they saw I had no life, they told my father to come in so he could say a prayer over my dead body. I could hear the Latin through the tears. His brother, my uncle, came into the room with him, he was smoking a cigar. He looked down at me for a long moment. And then my uncle grabbed my body, sucked on his cigar, put his mouth to mine . . . and blew! All that smoke, filling my lungs! I started to cough and cry and scream! I was breathing! The smoke brought me back to life! Men's smoke and women's tears! My father said it took Heaven and Hell to birth me, and he was right! Maybe that's why they pampered me, kept me in curls and bonnets and dresses. Pablito had everything but tits.

[**Miss Fischer**: "Pablito?"]

Picasso: Pablito Ruiz. Ruiz. Stupid, dull name. Like Smith or Duval or . . . Fischer. I got rid of it soon as I could. I took my mother's name. Picasso! Pablo Picasso! Looks better on the painting. Sounds better when you come into a room! My father always resented that. He'd say, "You are a Ruiz!" I'd say, "So is half of Spain."

When I was 8, my mother was with child again. Everyone was happy. "Oh, good! At last a brother for Pablito!" It was a girl. Her name was Maria de la Concepcion. Everyone was very unhappy, but not me. The first time I saw her . . . I fell in love. Her eyes, her curls. She'd watch me paint. I'd tell her, "Conchita, I am going to be a great painter. My paint and my brushes are my arms and my eyes." And she would say, "Yes, Pablo." Never "Pablito." To her I was always "Pablo."

Then Conchita got sick. The women prayed, the men prayed. But their prayers were beggars' prayers. "Please God! Pity her, God!" I knew even then if there was a God he was not like that. God does not respond to begging! God wants promises! God makes bargains! So I sneaked into Conchita's room one night. She was asleep, I could hear her little chest heave up and down. I went to the window and flung it open and knelt at the ledge, with my hands together and my eyes shut tight, like a good little Catholic boy. "God! Listen to me! My sister Conchita is dying. Make her well. Make her live. You do that . . . and I will give up painting. Forever."

The next day . . . *miracle!*. . . she begins to get better. Her breathing, her face! My beloved sister was getting well! I started to pack away my brushes, my paper. But I couldn't. They were my arms, my eyes. I could not put them away.

So I opened my own window . . . and I took back my bargain from God . . .

The next morning Conchita was dead. I went into her room and looked at her face. Cold and still, her hair flat with her sweat. So . . . I lit a match and let it burn to my fingers and then began to draw. I made her hair curly again. And I gave her her favorite bonnet. And I opened her eyes.

I hid the drawing in my room; I would never show it to anyone. But the day of the funeral, I found my father standing next to my bed, holding it in his hand. I was afraid. Did he know I had bargained my sister away? But all he said was . . . "I see you made a self-portrait." He thought it was me. Like you did.

THE PILGRIM PAPERS
BY STEPHEN TEMPERLEY

SQUANTO, *a flirtatious Native American with a Cockney accent, greets the recently arrived Pilgrims as they are about to celebrate Thanksgiving.*

SCENE
Plymouth

TIME
The 1620s

SQUANTO: Squanto's the name. But you can call me Phil.

[WINSLOW: How's this? The savage speaks English?

BRADFORD: (*Cautions him.*) Mr. Winslow. Sir . . .

WINSLOW: From whence comes such fluency? Is't sorcery? Or some enchantment?

SQUANTO: That's easily told, sunshine.] 'Twas like this. I was trollin' about the beach mindin' me own business—over there by that great big rock—when a slaver jumps up and grabs me. Next thing you know I'm in Malaga and he's sold me to an English lordship. Proper gent he was. Lovely manners, dead posh. Took me to London to be his . . . (*Searches for the word.*) companion. (*Winks at Ned in a conspiratorial manner.*) That was the life. Spoiled me rotten. Never wore nothing 'cept silk next to my skin. Look at me now! Rabbit and seashells! Anyway, we's on holiday in Torremolinos, Reg and me, when I pop in this place down by the beach for a quick pick-me-up and there's all these pirates playin' snooker. Well! We hit it off right away. Strawberry daiquiris flowin' like water. They're all showin' off their tattoos and flexin' their muscles and the next thing you know I wake up on board the *Bonny Buccaneer* bound for Tripoli. Lovely it was! Fresh flowers in the cabins, chocolates on your pillow, five-star dinners, everything first class. Anyway, we're cruisin' around, out past the Indies . . . Cathay . . . you name it . . . and on the way back they plan to stop off at Guyana—no, tell a lie, Santo Domingo—for a spot of pillage, when we get wrecked off the Tortugas. Turns out I'm the only one can swim. All the others went down with the ship. Singin' rude songs to the end. So. There I was, stuck on an island alone. Till a whaler stops off on his way to Greenland and offers me a lift. Ghastly ship. Fish guts everywhere. Frightful journey. And when I get home what do I find? All my lot's caught the measles off some buggery, bollocky sailors and snuffed it. So I'm the last of my kind! Always was, if you ask me. Pamets, we was. Part of the tribe of the Wampanoags. Allied with the Greater Iroquois Confederation.

(HE *gestures vaguely,* [*leaning heavily on Ned.*)]

They live that way. But you! What brings you here? I say, anyone fancy a toke? (*Offers his pipe around.*) No? It's good stuff. Don't worry. Got plenty more. Raised a super crop last year.

THE PILLOWMAN
BY MARTIN MCDONAGH

KATURIAN *is a writer in an unnamed totalitarian state who is being interrogated about the gruesome content of many of his stories and their similarities to a series of child murders. As* HE *reads what* HE *declares is his "best story,"* HE *enjoys his own words, its details, and its twists.*

SCENE
A police interrogation room

TIME
The present

KATURIAN: (*Pause.*) Um, 'Once upon a time in a tiny cobble-streeted town on the banks of a fast-flowing river, there lived a little boy who did not get along with the other children of the town; they picked on and bullied him because he was poor and his parents were drunkards and his clothes were rags and he walked around barefoot. The little boy, however, was of a happy and dreamy disposition, and he did not mind the taunts and the beatings and the unending solitude. He knew that he was kind-hearted and full of love and that someday someone somewhere would see this love inside him and repay him in kind. Then, one night, as he sat nursing his newest bruises at the foot of the wooden bridge that crossed the river and led out of town, he heard the approach of a horse and cart along the dark, cobbled street, and as it neared he saw that its driver was dressed in the darkest of robes, the black hood of which bathed his craggy face in shadow and sent a shiver of fear through the little boy's body. Putting his fear aside, the boy took out the small sandwich that was to be his supper that night and, just as the cart was about to pass onto and over the bridge, he offered it up to the hooded driver to see if he would like some. The cart stopped, the driver nodded, got down and sat beside the little boy for a while, sharing the sandwich and discussing this and that. The driver asked the boy why he was barefoot and ragged and all alone, and as the boy told the driver of his poor, hard life, he eyed the back of the driver's cart; it was piled high with small, empty animal cages, all foul-smelling and dirt-lined, and just as the boy was about to ask what kind of animals it was had been inside them, the driver stood up and announced that he had to be on his way. "But before I go," the driver whispered, "because you have been so kindly to an old weary traveller in offering half of your already meagre portions, I would like to give you something now, the worth of which today you may not realise, but one day, when you are a little older, perhaps, I think you will truly value and thank me for. Now close your eyes." And so the little boy did what he was told and closed his eyes, and from a secret inner pocket of his robes the driver pulled out a long, sharp and shiny meat cleaver, raised it high in the air and brought it scything down onto the boy's right foot, severing all five of his muddy little toes. And as the little boy sat there in gaping silent shock, staring blankly off into the distance at nothing in particular, the driver gathered up his bloody toes, tossed them away to the gaggle of rats that had begun to gather in the gutters, got back onto his cart, and quietly rode on over the bridge, leaving the boy, the rats, the river and the darkening town of *Hamelin* far behind him.'

PLATONOV!
PLATONOV! PLATONOV!
BY ERIC MICHAEL KOCHMER

In this satirical adaptation of an early Chekhov story, PLATONOV, *a village schoolmaster, is married to a "dumb sweet country girl." But* HE *loves all women and fears only age and death.*

SCENE
A Russian province

TIME
About 1881

PLATONOV: Wait! Don't go, Sofya Yagorovnachorgaforgagorgaforgab-orgachobia! Stay, please! Listen to me . . . I'm only just an ordinary schoolteacher. . . . Quack! Quack! Quack! that's all I've done since we we we last saw each other . . . but that is not my passion. What have I done for Platonov! Platonov! Platonov! I've married a dumb sweet country girl. . . . And now? I'm just a happy drunk duck mucking around in the same swamp I've already mucked around. . . . Soon I will be old!. . . only then I'll be a fat old worthless duck. My God, it's shocking! I open my eyes up and all I see is mediocrity all around me, plaguing the earth, swallowing up my fellow man, and yet I sit here, arms and body in a limbo static state. . . . I sit and watch in the dark of silence with the rest of my friends and say and do nothing . . . and one day I'll be 40 . . . and nothing will change. I'll still walk around as the same fool I am today and with the same dumb wife and the same women will be falling at my feet . . . one day I'll be 50 . . . one day I'll be 60 . . . one day I'll be 70 . . . 80 . . . 90 . . . 100 — dead on the ground, dust in the earth — and nothing will ever change for me . . . nothing will ever change . . . I will always be lusting around . . . no change in the horizon . . . and meanwhile I grow into a fat and dull and idle duck . . . my feathers are ruffled and one day I'll just be skin. . . . My life is lost. . . . All of my ambitions, all of my passions lost! The life of this duck wasted. . . . I am impotent to intellect and substantial opinions. . . . What is left? What is left? My feathers prick to the touch when I think of my death. . . . My feathers prick to the touch when I think of my death. . . . My feathers prick to the touch when I think of my death . . . death . . . death. . . . Oh Sofya, what have I done! What have I done!

[Sofya: I can't bear this any longer, take me now!

Platonov: Ha! Ha! Ha! I love women! Quack! Quack! Quack!]

PROPHECY

BY KAREN MALPEDE

JEREMY *is working class, and an acting student who threw a chair into a mirror midway through a monologue from Antigone by Sophocles. Later, we find out* HE *is an Iraq war vet. The play is about how the wars of the twenty-first century enter the lives of ordinary people.*

SCENE

His acting teacher Sarah Golden's living room in the middle of the night. JEREMY *has come to her house to explain what triggered his behavior in class, although* HE *doesn't tell her about the war until a later scene.*

TIME

The summer of 2006

JEREMY: Yeah, okay, I will tell you. I was doing the speech of the prophet, see. Tiresias' speech, the blind guy, and he's giving this prophecy when all of a sudden, he's saying that the fat isn't burning, that the altars are glutted with the fat thigh bones smoking, that the gods aren't hearing, that they won't take the offering in. And that's when it hits me, shit, fuck, like a truck, it hits. We've been cut off. We're floating free in space and even the gods aren't listening; they don't care anymore. We've gone too far. They won't take our offerings. I'm a Catholic. I was brought up to believe in forgiveness. In redemption, see. You say you're sorry. You say you've sinned. It's okay. God forgives you. You say twenty Hail Marys and you're back in. He's a forgiving god. But all of a sudden I think it might not work that way, you see what I mean? It might work another way. You might go too far. You might step off the end of the earth. There might be no way back. The altars might be glutted with flesh. And that's when I saw, like I didn't see out of my eyes. I was blind. I saw it inside my head. How it is when the gods can't bear to listen. They can't bear to hear anymore. They've already heard it all. You can't ask for forgiveness. The gods aren't hearing. They're fed up with us, sick. We're cut off. I got scared.

THE PROPOSAL
BY TIM MILLER

The performer, MAN, *recalls an incident from his childhood when honesty was not necessarily the best policy regarding gender preference in a marriage partner.* HE *plays all parts.*

SCENE
The stage

TIME
The present looking to the past

MAN: It was a day of judgmental Twinkies being smashed in my face. I was 9 years old. I was walking down Russell Street with my friend Scott, he was a second cousin of President Richard Nixon and we lived in Whittier, the president's hometown. So you can see, Republicans have been fucking with me for as long as I can remember. We walked, free-associating as young boys will do. We walked by a house that was widely regarded as the most tasteful in our neighborhood, much respected for its impressive series of ceramic elves decorating the winding walkway to the front door!

Scott said to me, "When I grow up, I'm going to marry that cute girl in our class, Gail Gardener, and we're gonna live in that house with the ceramic elves." Then Scott looked at me as if he thought he deserved a ninety-nine and a happy face on a spelling test.

This was a new subject and I sensed that it meant trouble. I bought some time and walked silently along, my *Lost in Space* lunch box clanking against my leg. My *Lost in Space* lunch box filled with my favorite lunch. A sandwich, made with Wonder Bread of course, and layers of delicious Jif smooth peanut butter and Welch's grape jelly with a generous crunchy handful of Fritos corn chips in between. (MMM, all that delicious sugar, oil and salt! Everything a young American needs to grow strong.) Next to my thermos was a special treat: a Twinkie in its crisp, confident plastic wrapper.

I knew I was making a mistake before I even opened my mouth. "But, Scott, when I grow up, I want to marry you and live in the house with the ceramic elves!" He looked at me as if I suggested that we tap dance together to the moon.

"What! Boys can't get married to each other. Everybody knows that."

"Why not?"

"They just can't."

"Why?"

"Because."

"Because why?"

Clearly, logic wasn't working so Scott pushed me hard with both hands, knocking me into the deep dusty ivy of my Congregationalist minister's front yard. We all knew rats lurked and prospered in the dark gnarly labyrinth of the ancient ivy. I drowned in the dirty green.

Scott jumped on me, looking around to see if anyone had heard me ask him to marry me. "Take it back! Say you don't want to marry me and live in the house with the elves!"

"I won't take it back!"

"Take it back, or I'll give you an Indian burn." He pinched my side hard and then grabbed my wrist with both hands and twisted in opposite directions. He screamed, "Do you take it back?"

"I won't take it back!"

He Indian-burned my other wrist. I probably could have fought him off. I wasn't that much of a wuss, but part of me had longed for some kind of closeness with Scott ever since kindergarten. Being tortured by him would have to do. You've all been there. My lunch box had fallen open near my head, revealing the Twinkie in all its cellophane splendor. Scott got a horrible idea and grabbed the Twinkie in his little fist.

"Take it back or I'm going to jam this Twinkie in your throat and kill you!"

"I won't take it back!" The strength of my high-pitched voice surprised me. "When I grow up, I'm going to marry you and live in the house with the ceramic elves!"

A look of shock and frustration passed like bad weather across Scott's face. He shoved the Twinkie into my mouth and held his small dirty palm over my lips. I exploded with cellophane and

Twinkie goo. Now, even more than climbing into boxes with lids, I knew kids weren't supposed to suck on cellophane. I took the warnings on the dry-cleaning bags seriously. I knew I'd reached my Twinkie limit and I would have to take it back. Fortunately, my oldest brother had just taught me the week before a special trick. Whenever anyone is tormenting you and wanting you to be untrue to yourself and take something back, all you have to do is cross your fingers and put them behind your back. This erases it. In case you thought this stopped working in childhood, it didn't. It still works in adult life, especially around relationship issues! I quickly crossed my fingers behind my back.

"All right! I take it back." Scott got off of me. He looked so strange. He kicked me, grabbed his math book and banal *Bonanza* lunch box, and stormed off to school and the rest of his life filled with petty disappointments and three wives who would fear him. (Don't ask me how, I just know!)

I lay there on my back, pinned to the earth. Surrounded by primordial ivy dust and Twinkie. I pulled my crossed fingers from underneath my back and held them up to the sky. The crossing of those fingers negated my "I take it back," my one triumph over his small tyranny. I held them up to the hot California sun as I repeated the words—they gathered steam inside me. "I will never take it back. I will never take it back. I will never take it back."

RABBIT HOLE

BY DAVID LINDSAY-ABAIRE

In this letter, JASON, *a 17-year-old, tries to explain his feelings to the parents of the young boy* HE *accidentally killed with his car.*

SCENE
Larchmont, New York

TIME
The present

JASON: Dear Mr. and Mrs. Corbett,

I wanted to send you my condolences on the death of your son, Danny. I know it's been eight months since the accident, but I'm sure it's probably still hard for you to be reminded of that day. I think about what happened a lot, as I'm sure you do, too. I've been having some troubles at home, and at school, and a couple people here thought it might be a good idea to write to you. I'm sorry if this letter upsets you. That's obviously not my intention.

Even though I never knew Danny, I did read that article in the town paper, and was happy to learn a little bit about him. He sounds like he was a great kid. I'm sure you miss him a lot, as you said in the article. I especially liked the part where Mr. Corbett talked about Danny's robots, because when I was his age I was a big fan of robots, too. In fact I still am, in some ways — ha ha.

I've enclosed a short story that's going to be printed in my high school lit magazine. I don't know if you like science fiction or not, but I've enclosed it anyway. I was hoping to dedicate the story to Danny's memory. There aren't any robots in this one, but I think it would be the kind of story he'd like if he were my age. Would it bother you if I dedicated the story? If so, please let me know. The printer deadline for the magazine is March 31st. If you tell me before then, I can have them take it off.

I know this probably doesn't make things any better, but I wanted you to know how terrible I feel about Danny. I know that no matter how hard this has been on me, I can never understand the depth of your loss. My mom has only told me that about a hundred times — ha ha. I of course wanted to say how sorry I am that things happened the way they did, and that I wish I had driven down a different block that day. I'm sure you do, too.

Anyway, that's it for now. If you'd like to let me know about the dedication, you can email me at the address above. If I don't hear from you, I'll assume it's okay.

Sincerely, Jason Willette

THE REBIRTH
BY LISA SOLAND

SAMUEL *is a typical workaholic in his late 20s or early 30s. He has just learned who his birth mother is and has inadvertently met her as well. He speaks directly to the audience.*

SCENE
A hearing room in Washington, D.C.

TIME
The present

SAMUEL: My birth mother.

(*It settles in.*)

My birth mother?

(*Beat.*)

How did you do that? How did you find her? Do you have any idea how hard that is? I've been looking for her for, I don't know . . . three years now. Who are you people? That's it, isn't it?

(*Rises, crosses downstage to audience.*)

You're with the government, aren't you? You must be, because no one could do that any faster than me, her own son, for God's sake. Jesus Christ. If it's that easy, why don't you do it for everybody? Huh?! Why don't you guys do it for everybody and earn those tax dollars we keep handing you on a fucking silver platter! Do you realize how many kids are searching desperately for their birth parents? Some never find them. I was afraid I wasn't going to. . . . Where is she? Is she . . .

(*Crosses stage right and points towards the door.*)

Was that her?

(*Beat.*)

Oh God, I gotta sit down. Do you mind?

(*Sits on the edge of stage, downstage right.*)

This is awful what you people do. You can't mess with people's lives like this. Where did you find her? Alaska? Because it's the only state I didn't look.

(*Looking up at audience, directly, with determination.*)

Yet.

(*Beat.*)

Is she okay?

(*Begins to loosen tie.*)

I'm having a hard time breathing here.

(*Removes tie.*)

So, are you going to bring her in here or what, because I've got to lie down or something. I'm not feeling too well.

(*Lies back on the stage floor.*)

[**HARRIS:** Excuse me. (*Stands and moves toward exit, calling out.*) Laurie?

LAURIE: (*Offstage.*) Yes.

HARRIS: (*Offstage.*) Could you get me some water?

LAURIE: (*Offstage.*) Sure.

(*Harris re-enters, sitting back in same seat.*)]

SAMUEL: (*From lying position.*) You know, they took me away, right after I was born. I know that now because after the rebirth in Seal Beach, I called the hospital in Cincinnati and they described it to me in detail. They weren't going to tell me at first. I had to get rough.

[(*Laurie enters with water and is not sure whom to give it to. Harris motions to* SAMUEL. *She hands it to* HIM.)

SAMUEL: Thank you. (HE *looks up to see that it's Laurie.* HE *quickly rises, brushes off his pants, leaving tie on floor.*) Oh, Laurie! Thank you very much.

(*Laurie smiles and exits.* SAMUEL *drinks nearly the entire bottle, while watching Laurie leave.*)]

Samuel: (*Crossing to chair,* He *sits.*) Don't you think that's unfair? They took me away. I should have been held by her. I should have been up against my mother's bosom. I needed to hear her heartbeat. I needed to hear the thing that I'd been hearing for the past nine months, in that safe, quiet place. People don't realize how important this is. "Be a man." Well, I don't want to be a man anymore. I want to be a HUMAN BEING.

(*Beat.*)

It affects your whole life, those first few moments out here in the open, and they stole that away from me. They stole that away from me and I needed to know that this place, out here, was safe too. I needed to know that. I needed to hear her heartbeat!

RED ROSES
BY LISA SOLAND

ROBERT, *30 to 45 years old, is a work-at-home father, frustrated and angry about his wife's receiving a bouquet of red roses.* HE *confronts her with his suspicions.*

SCENE
The living room

TIME
The present

ROBERT: "This is not like me at all." "This is not like me at all?!" Guess what else is "not like me at all?" Running this house is "not like me," that's what. Directing traffic at the crosswalk. Driving the kids from school to field hockey, to home, to Scottie's, is "not like me at all." I am tired of pancake batter and wiping up their faces and then the floor. And when I finally have a moment to myself, to sand, to work, to do what it is I am put on this earth to do, which I should be doing at the studio . . .

(*Corrects himself.*)

Workshop.

(*Continuing, even more angry.*)

The doorbell rings and it's the "completion of the tender passion." Now, what does the card say, Julie?

(*Beat.*)

"Happy birthday, Sweetheart." Oh. Okay. And you don't know who they're from?

(*Louder.*)

And you don't know who they're from?

(*Beat. Retrieves cordless phone.*)

Ya know what? I'm going to call that publisher-guy-friend of yours and have a little chat. What's his name?

(*Beat.*)

What's his name?

(*Beat.*)

You know which one—the guy with the oiled hair, and the suspenders with the matching socks. The one who for some strange reason volunteers to take you to the airport every time you need to go anywhere because you've got to sign books on the way. That "which one."

(*Beat.*)

Darryl! What's the number?

(Robert *dials as Julie dictates from memory.* He *then looks at his watch.*)

He'd never be back to the office this quickly . . . or is that his home number?

(*She does not respond.* He *hangs up the phone.*)

Okay.

(Robert *exits into bedroom. After a moment he re-enters with an arm full of pressed jeans, shirts on hangers and a canvas overnight bag.* He *sets all items on couch and begins to pack, grappling with well-starched and pressed blue jeans on hangers.* He *holds them out to her.*)

I don't want my jeans sent to the cleaners. Okay? I want them thrown into the washer and then the dryer and then folded and put into a regular drawer made out of strong, sturdy wood. I don't care how much money you're making. I never did anything for the money. There was a time, a very happy time, when we had none. I don't want pleats or this bullshit. Do you hear me?

(*Handing her the* Blooming Implications *book, left open.*)

I've put up with all these stupid little things, these things that somehow make you feel as though you're successful in life because I had the most important thing of all—you. I had you. Now that that's not mine anymore, don't . . .

(*Cutting off her interruption.*)

Now that that's not mine anymore, DON'T PRESS MY JEANS!!!

(*Jams clothes into canvas bag, exits front door.*)

SHYNESS IS NICE

BY MARC SPITZ

FITZGERALD *is a brand new junkie, trying to lose his "nice guy" image.* HE *wears a shiny black suit and has spiked hair.* HE *is frantically searching for something while suppressing a severe asthma attack.*

SCENE
A small New York City apartment littered with books and records, mostly Beat literature and jazz

TIME
The present

(*The phone rings. It rings and rings again.* FITZGERALD *stops, tries to calm his breathing. Walks over to the record player and puts on some jazz. Lights a cigarette. Pauses. Finally* HE *picks it up.*)

FITZGERALD: (*Super cool voice.*) This is Fitzgerald. (*Quick beat/long pant/complete crack in cool façade.*) Hello? (*Beat.*) Mommy? (HE *extinguishes the smoke, takes the record off the turntable.*) Help me, Mommy. (*More panting.*) I can't find it. My inhaler! Listen to me! (*Wheezes.*) I'm having an attack. (HE *continues to search while panting into the phone, finds some porno mags under pillows.*) Mommy! Can you help me, please? Well, bring me a new one. I know you're on Long Island, but I'm dying. I am *too* dying. I can't breathe. Please? I'm very scared. (*Beat/call waiting.*) Oh, wait. Hang on. (HE *places the needle on the jazz again. Relights the cigarette. Regains cool. Smooth/cool.*) This is Fitzgerald. (*Beat.*) Mom? Shit, hang on. (*Clicks the receiver madly/smooth cool voice.*) Fitzgerald. Who? Blixa. Yeah, I remember you. Shit, baby, it was just last night. Yeah I'm still interested in the deal. Say what? Oh, yeah. No problem. Leave it to me. As long as you're cool, I'm cool. Don't worry 'bout it. Yeah, ha ha. You know it. All right. All right. Ciao, baby. (*Clicks/wheezes.*) Mommy? (*Extinguishes cigarette. Continues to rummage. Finds pill bottle. Unscrews it. Swallows pills.*) No, Mommy, I'm not going over there. No, Mommy, Aunt Susan scares me. No, Mommy, I'm not doing that either. No! Have you ever tried to wait on line for anything at CVS? No, Mommy. Mommy, will you let me talk? Will you please let me talk? Will you . . . will you let me. . . . Thank you. (*Swallows more pills.*) I'm fine. I'm fine. No . . . it wasn't an asthma attack. No. It was a panic attack. Okay. Okay. No. All right. I will. I promise. Okay. Mommy? Will you send me some food? Thanks. I love you too. Night night. (*Clicks receiver/lights cigarette/changes again.*) This is Fitzgerald! Hey, what's shakin' baby? Me? Just doing my thing. Yeah. Hey, dig this, right? I got a major surprise for you. Yeah, yeah, the both of you. Shit, man, if I spilled over the phone, it wouldn't be a major surprise, now, would it. All right. Yeah, I'll meet you there. Be cool. Me? Always cool, baby, you know that. (*Beat/anger.*) I am too. I *am not* talking funny. Fuck off. Maybe I won't come over, Rodney. (*Beat.*) All right . . . but watch it. (*Hangs up phone.*) Yeah, you better watch your ass. (*Paces apartment. Puts on shades.*) Or I'll . . . kick it.

SMALL DOMESTIC ACTS
BY JOAN LIPKIN

FRANK, *good-natured blue-collar guy, confides in his friend and co-worker Frankie, a lesbian, that his wife Sheila has suddenly started getting angry over little things. In fact, Sheila is falling in love with Frankie's partner, and she will leave* FRANK *for her.* FRANK *eventually apologizes to his wife for making TV dinners when it was his turn to cook, or tries to.*

SCENE
The stage

TIME
The present

FRANK: (*Beat. To Frankie.*) She's always angry these days. I didn't know it when we were first together. Because she was sweet then. I guess we were both on good behavior. You know, polite. Asking which movie the other one wanted to see. And now, there is all this anger. I feel a little cheated. Like she is not the girl she made herself out to be. (*To the audience.*) Sometimes, it scares the hell out of me. And the littlest things set her off. Things I don't even care about. She didn't used to be like this. Or maybe I just didn't know. She says she's been changing. And the older she gets, (*Mimicking Straight Sheila.*) the less bullshit she wants to put up with. And moody. God, is she moody. Now, me? I'm just regular all the time. The same. What you see is what you get. (*Beat.*) For a while I thought, this is for the birds. Who needs this? I can find myself someone else. Somebody nice and sweet and uncomplicated. And then I thought, how? And where? And I didn't want to have to get comfortable with someone else again. (*Beat.*) Most of the time, it's pretty good. I love sleeping with her and she does nice things for me sometimes. She'll pick up a movie I want to see or make something special for dinner. She won't pick up my shirts from the cleaners, though, and she gets mad if I ask her. I don't get it. I mean, what's the difference between picking up my shirts or picking up a movie? But I'll tell you something. Maureen, my last girlfriend? She never got angry. And she was pretty. I was never as hot for her like I am for Sheila, but it was okay. It was comfortable. We had the house and we had our friends and in the beginning, she used to bake all the time. Just like my mom. I'd come home and the house would smell like chocolate. But one day, she came home and said she wanted out. Just like that. I wanted to work it out. I even said I'd go see someone and I don't go in for that kind of bullshit. But she said it was too far gone. Too much had happened that she couldn't live with. So now, even though I don't understand it and it sometimes makes me crazy, I'll take Sheila's anger any day. Besides, with someone else, if it wasn't this, it would be something else. (*To Straight Sheila.*) Okay, so maybe I should have made something else for dinner. Next time, I'll bake a ham. Or roast a friggin' turkey with all the trimmings. (*To the audience.*) She can pretend that it's Thanksgiving.

SOME GIRL(S)
BY NEIL LABUTE

In his 30s and engaged, Guy *reconnects with Bobbi, an old girlfriend, to try and convince her that she is the only one* He *really loves.* He *was tape-recording the meeting in hopes that she will give* Him *material for a short story. She does not fall for his ruse.*

SCENE
A hotel room

TIME
The present

Guy: Fine, yes, you got me! You smoked me out, so bully for you. I sometimes use the people around me to further my career . . . well, Bobbi, that makes me an American, frankly, and that is about it. Look, I'm not even one of those authors who're out there right now pretending like all their shit is real or, or . . . hiding behind the persona of some 12-year-old *boy*—I don't do any of that! I am just me and I write amusing stories while changing the names of everybody involved and I don't see who's getting hurt by it. I really don't. (*Beat.*) I'm not, like, you know . . . doing this all *haphazardly* or anything. It's, it's . . . for *Esquire*! Just because I'm an author doesn't mean I'm not able to have human . . . *stuff*. I can't help it if I'm complex. (*Beat.*) Does that make me some big, despicable creature just because I continue to search? To reach out for my happiness on a profoundly human level? I don't think so. I'm not sick, Bobbi. I am not evil. I may be a bunch of things, but I'm not that. . . . And I'm not trying to take anything away from what I did, I am not—I did such a . . . stupid, stupid thing back so many years ago, and I'm *sorry*. I could try and place blame on something else, say it's a horrible age we live in now, a world that doesn't give two shits about other people's feelings and where folks sit up until *four* in the morning searching for sex on the Internet while a loved one is sleeping fifty feet away . . . or some guy will *text-message* his wife to say, "I'm leaving you." All of these little atrocities that we visit on each other that are really pretty breathtaking. (*Beat.*) But I can't. That's not the problem. *This* was my fault, all of it. I was just young and dumb and, I dunno, goofy and, you know—those were my *good* qualities!. . . I'm a guy, I'm bad at this, Bobbi; I found the single greatest person I could ever imagine being near, I mean *standing* near, even, and she liked me. Me! And that just didn't compute, it did not make sense, no matter what she said to me . . . so I made myself believe it wasn't true and I ran off. Like some 3-year-old. (*Beat.*) But I've grown up since then, I have—all this being with other women and writing about it and telling myself that I should go visit my past before I marry . . . I realize now, it's all about *you*! I don't care if you buy it or hate me or laugh in my face. . . . (*Tears up a bit.*) I love you and I'm . . . oh, boy. No way I'm gonna top that, so I'll just leave off right there. I love, you Bobbi. Not your sister, not anybody else I've ever known, even this girl I'm supposed to marry . . . no one. Just you.

SOUVENIR
BY STEPHEN TEMPERLEY

The accompanist to singer Florence Foster Jenkins, COSIMO MCMOON *is a dapper man in his late 50s sitting at a piano.* HE *is amazed, but also concerned, that the singer, who is phenomenally bad, has been able to generate enthusiastic audiences.*

SCENE
The club

TIME
The 1930s

COSIMO MCMOON: It was like magic. Word just spread.

Every time she sang more people wanted to hear. You couldn't keep them away. (HE *rises to stand in the curve of the piano.*) As word got around the audience changed. It wasn't just her Park Avenue friends anymore. It was more like the crowd you see at the fights. We were at the Ritz-Carlton, so there was a certain level of restraint. Even so I'd see them crying. When she sang. Doubled over in their seats. Hitting each other, convulsed. There were gasps, sudden shrieks. They'd jump to their feet and run up the aisles. You'd hear doors banging. And the sound from the lobby of people laughing. When they got themselves under control they'd make their way back to their seats, flushed, still wiping tears away. You see a lot from a piano bench. Meanwhile, Madame Flo was lost in the music. So far as she was concerned the people running for the doors were just too moved to stay. Too overcome by emotion.

(*Returning to the bench.*) At the end there were bravos and flowers. And afterwards she'd serve sherry and her friends would talk about what she wore. So one way or another everyone had a pretty good time. (HE *pauses, troubled.*) Though I worried. In case a day might come when the balance tipped, when her friends were outnumbered by that other, crueler part of the audience. When the ones coming to laugh set the tone.

SPIN

BY RANDY WYATT

In his 30s, CARVER *finds the courage and trust to reveal his magical talent to his lover.*

SCENE
At a table

TIME
Now, late in the evening

CARVER: You can ask my mother. She's the only other one I've let see me do it.

I was in my playpen, 4 years old. She says she saw me wiggle my fingers—I won't do it now—and she saw my teddy twirl around, like it was in an invisible dryer. And she screamed and told me to do it again, honey, do it again. But she scared me, I thought I was in trouble, see. So I didn't. And later on, she'd say she was seeing things, but she'd say it with this penetrating look at me, as if she were asking me a question but couldn't find the words. That's how young I was when I knew.

At first it was great. I mean, just a thrill. I'd duck out of school early and run to the park, sit on the bench and make pigeons dizzy. A quick twirl—oops, haha, almost did it again—twirl my fingers and sort of blow. The blow was for dramatic effect, because I know it's all in the fingers but I can feel—I mean, I can actually feel the tiny currents, like little threads, wrapping around my fingers, and some sort of electric tingle on the tips, the very tips of my fingers—and then a little flick, and I send it off. This little cyclone. And it spins and it spins and then . . . it's gone. Just a couple of seconds. Like the water whorls you see when the water goes down the drain. Little vortexes. All mine.

Sometimes I thought I was dreaming it, I mean, I was a dreamy kid. I'd even force myself to forget about it for a while, because parents and teachers and everybody—they teach you to be, you know, normal. But I couldn't forget this, of course, I mean, I could do this amazing thing that nobody else could do. Then I thought that maybe this power would grow, and I was gonna be a superhero. Tornado Man. So I started "training." Asked my old man for a punching bag. He was so happy. Slung it up in the cellar, and I'd go down there, punch it a few times, barely make the thing move, and then wiggle my fingers and watch this tiny whirlwind fly from my hand, boomerang back into my hair and knock my own glasses off. Oh, but I'd dream, ya know? I'd dream that someday I'd be huge and mighty, and hurl F-fives at the bad guys and whisk them off to jail. But no matter how I twisted or flailed my arms around, they never got bigger. (He *makes a wimpy whooshing sound.*) That's all I could do. Just these little dust devils, five, maybe six inches tall. Pathetic.

When I figured this out, I was a teenager, and I just felt stupid about it. The way you feel stupid about everything.

And I didn't really do it again until . . . years after college. I tried to just erase it from my mind and go on, because it wasn't worth anything, because it didn't mean anything, I mean, little cyclones? What good are they? Who cares? Like my father said about painting. I tried to take a course in it once but my father scoffed. "What good will that do ya? College ain't recess." So I dropped it and went on. Because life ain't recess. And that became my mantra with everything. "What's it good for?"

But I care. I admit it. I think it's beautiful. I can't explain it and I think that's the best part. I don't want to know how I do it. I just know I can.

And now you know. You're the only person I've ever told. You inspire me. You make me want to tell you things, to bare my soul. And now you know my two innermost secrets. First, that loving you — trusting you — feels like jumping off a mountain, I mean, like being tossed in a hurricane, it scares me that much, exhilarates me that much. And this.

I don't want to be ashamed of either anymore.

I watch my father die nightly. He takes so many pills and he's strong for his age but his skin is like parchment in some library somewhere. Flaking. You know it's just a matter of time. And it just makes me realize — looking at him, it makes me realize that these secrets of mine — they shouldn't be. I should be so much more visible than I've ever allowed myself.

That's the spin I put on it, anyway.

Maybe I'll tell him. Let him see what it's good for.

You wanna see it, don't you? (He *nods.*) All right. Take my hand.

One. Two. No more secrets.

(He *raises his arm. The lights go out.*)

Three.

STORYTELLERS

BY THOMAS MCCORMACK

BREN *is a fit, even athletic, Irish-American without a brogue;* HE *wouldn't look out of place on an oil rig or a construction site.* HE *has quite a brilliant academic career, and* HE*'s now secluded* HIMSELF *to try to become a writer.* HE *seems insulated, distanced, by courtesy and a guarded poise devoid of jiggles and sawing the air. His modest clothes are from L.L. Bean. Here,* HE*'s speaking to Elga, a smart, sympathetic book editor who has also been his landlady. She's been trying to understand this extraordinary young man.* HE *has just told her* HE *is going away.*

SCENE
A one-room studio apartment on the beach side of a large home on the shore of the Long Island Sound in Stamford, Connecticut, thirty-five miles from New York City

TIME
Now

BREN: (HE *holds a can of soda water.* HE *gazes at it, unopened, pondering.* HE *will from time to time seem to contemplate the can, revolve it slowly in the reflecting light, read it as though seeing a message there.* HE *does all this with a sober maturity;* HE *is not a child playing with a toy. Only near the end, when* HE *announces his decision, does* HE *finally pop the can open.*)

You do ask lots of questions: why I quit, why I'm going home, why I say I'm a disappointer, why I want . . . remoteness. I'll try to give honest answers, but I won't trust them. You shouldn't either: never trust autobio. A writer will self-justify, self-compliment, lie.

One writer I know explained why his sister despises him.

("*Sympathetically.*")

"I only asked her what her hopes were for her short story."

What he really asked was,

(*Sneering.*)

"What's a tone-deaf, semi-illiterate like you think you can possibly do with shit like this?"

Don't let anything I'm about to say convince you I'm a fountain of compassion. I'm not. For example, at the first sign of *needy* in someone, I want to run like hell. If I let someone come to depend on me, I'll feel *hooked*. It's a defect, but it's not unique to me. Very few primary caregivers do it with unsullied whole-heartedness. We wish . . .

Also: You ever run low on *disdain*, apply to me. It used to yellow up in me like combustible sulfur whenever I met self-confident fools—and I felt they came on in battalions—at grad school and then when I taught seminars at Oxford. Lots of remoteness justified right there.

You look at my academic record, and my reputation in philosophy, and the so-called ultra-high IQ scores, and you say, "C'mon Bren! Why all the self-deprecation! It's silly!" I was part of a forty-year study of ultras at Princeton. We learned a high score entails only that you're pretty good at a *range* of different things. It doesn't imply you're world-class at anything.

So it's not self-deprecating for me to believe there are things I can't do! In particular, things I can't do for *people*. *Some* people. *Most* people. One way or another I disappoint. It'd be senseless not to admit it! Above all, don't try to cast me as a super-modest guy mewing, "Poor me, I disappoint because I'm just not good enough—" That's not me.

At Princeton, there were classes graded on a curve. I saw guys come to the door on day one, see I was in the class and say, "The hell with this," and go register for something else where they figured their chances were better. Somehow, it did not make me giggle.

But those guys I don't bleed for. The awful thing is disappointing kind people, good people, and I do that: women, benefactors, philosophers. At Oxford a generous, decent man on the faculty took me under his wing, became a comrade. We used to have dinner together, smoke cigars together. He wrote an important scholarly paper about "truth-conditions," everyone was high on it, it was about to be published. One night, over a glass of port, I made a mistake: I showed *him* a mistake in his theory, a basic flaw. His most ambitious paper . . . was wrong. I didn't mention it to anyone else, but he *withdrew* the paper, and it was never the same after that, with him. Disappointment hung in the air like the smell of urine. Our dinners soon stopped.

You wonder if I don't regret leaving philosophy, and why I won't say I was good at it. Okay: I was *wickedly* good. A famous man once said *vanity* is a necessity in a philosopher. I had it—and I grew to hate it. But hating your bad traits doesn't kill them—they seem to *thrive* on the attention.

No — I don't regret leaving philosophy. I left for the same reason some people quit Wall Street, or defending criminals they know are guilty, or even selling insurance. They quit because they *despise themselves for doing it*! They know the awful feeling of seeing yourself be *gorgeously, hideously clever.*

Here's how I sounded. I was on an Internet philosophy forum, and there was an anti-American bigot in Paris who was such a constant fool I finally wrote him this, online: "People say either you plagiarize your thinking from an utter fool, or you're stone-stupid all on your own. In your defense, I tell everyone it's wrong and *unkind* to say you plagiarize."

In other subjects you triumph by adding something new. In philosophy, triumph requires slaying someone old, proving them wrong. At my worst, I'd feel a gladiator's glee. There are many decent philosophers. I wasn't one.

(*Pops the can open; his tone changes, as though moving on to another subject.*)

So that's why I'm going back to Galway. I'll be living in the house where my grandfather, my mother, and I were all born, and where I lived for my first two years, before my mother took me to America. I'm told I'll inherit it one day — the house, the beach, and the echoes.

Over there, the best Irish dancers are treated like prima ballerinas, and my mother . . . could have been *the best in the world.* She lost it all because of me. Now, in that old, memory-wracked house, I have a job to do. My mother had a somber fear she'd be forgotten, but that's one disappointment I'll spare her. I don't know how well, but I *will* write her story: She *will be remembered*, at least for a time, at least by a few of us.

Whatever happens, given my wondrous aptitudes I figure I can still make it as a high-school teacher in some rural village on the Irish coast. . . .

TALES OF AN URBAN INDIAN

BY DARRELL DENNIS

At 22, SIMON, *a Canadian Indian, recalls attending an integrated junior high in Vancouver, dealing with racism, and his inevitable attraction to the "Forbidden Fruit," a.k.a. white girls.*

SCENE
Wolves Lake Reservation, British Columbia. The words "Forbidden Fruit" appear on the projection screen.

TIME
The play begins in 1972 and spans twenty-two years. In this monologue, SIMON *is talking about events that occurred in 1985 when* HE *was 13.*

SIMON: By the start of the eighth grade I was catching the bus to attend junior high. It would get to the reserve at 7:30 AM, and for about an hour there was fun for Natives of all ages. Then the bus would arrive in town and we would pull into the golf course where the rich white kids lived. All the Natives would fall silent and move to the back of the bus. If you listened closely, you could hear Rosa Parks cussing us out. Then, a sea of blonde hair, designer clothes, and an overpowering smell of perfume would flood the bus. The master race. Any brown person trapped in a seat beside a white person was the focus of the tribe.

[**Nick:** Tommy's in a window seat beside a white one!

Simon, Age 13: You stay here. I'm going in to get him.

Nick: For the love of God, man. No sudden movements. They can smell fear.

Simon, Age 13: Dammit! We got Math together. I'm not leaving him behind.]

Simon: It was us against them, even though none of them knew we existed. Except when they had to sit beside one of us. They would turn up their noses and roll their eyes. When we finally got to school it was just more of the same. Indians against whites. Rich against poor. Everybody against the East Indians. You could walk from one end of the hall to the next and hear all the nations of the world slammed between periods. "Honky," "Wagon-burner," "Chink," "Paki," "Wop," "Kike," "Spade." Everyone stayed with their own, the status quo was maintained, and everybody was expected to be content. That's when I started to crave the forbidden fruit. The white girls at my school seemed so pure. They didn't walk down the hall, they floated, and little cartoon animals would flock around them. They had it all. They were living the life we saw on TV. Where every problem was solved in twenty-two minutes. The apple of my eye was Kimberly Thompson. She had big, pouty lips, she wore an adult-sized bra, and she came from Viking stock. I found her name in the phonebook and with my best pal Nick beside me, I was about to break on through to the other side. . . . I dialled the number. My heart was pounding through my chest. My face was burning. Nick was standing in front of me, breathing his beef-jerky breath in my face. One ring. "Oh God, please don't be home." Two rings. "Please God, don't let her be home." Three rings. "Thank you, God." Click.

THEY'RE JUST LIKE US

BY BOO KILLEBREW

Once the lover of a young actress who is now famous, RICHARD *has moved on.* HE *gives a "pretend" interview to Barbara Walters, perhaps looking in a mirror.*

SCENE
Indoors

TIME
The present

RICHARD: No, I don't really like to do interviews. I figure, you're Barbara Walters, so if I ever am going to do an interview, this would be the one to do. (*Listens.*) Yes, people do still ask me about her. A lot, actually—photographers everywhere, calling my mother, following me into the public bathroom—all that stuff. (*Listens.*) I'm great actually. I teach drama to high school students and I'm married to a wonderful woman and I have a backyard and a dog and lots of wide open space. (*Listens.*) Yes, I hear she's doing that. I'm sure it will be absolutely wonderful, she's really a very talented character actress. (*Listens.*) I called it off, yes. I just couldn't really stand that kind of lifestyle any longer. It's not me. (*Listens.*) We don't really talk anymore, no. (*Listens.*) I do miss her, Barbara. We used to have a really good time together. I miss her feet, she had great feet. (*Loses focus.*) I miss sitting in the audience, watching her onstage, and knowing that she would go home with me that night. I miss the way she would smile with her lips closed. I miss how quiet she would get every time it would rain. I miss her trying to hide pictures of herself in my sock drawer. I miss her blinking. (*Snaps out of it.*) Yes, I would say that there are times when I wonder if I made the right decision, but then I remember how she was one of those women that you just can't keep. I was always looking at her and she was always looking out. (*Stops the interview.*) This is stupid. I am so stupid.

THIRD PERSON
BY PETER S. PETRALIA

This play follows the strange love affair of two ordinary men whose brushes with loneliness, death, and madness frame their attraction to one another. CHARACTER A *narrates a story* HE *once read about a man who had no sensory feelings of heat or cold or pain.* A *became obsessed with finding the man and kissing him.*

SCENE
A stage with two microphones placed opposite each other

TIME
The present

CHARACTER A: I read a news story once about a man who couldn't feel heat or cold or pain. He grew up getting cut and not crying, walking in the snow and not freezing, stepping in fire and not even noticing. His body was a riddle of scars from the burns, lacerations and frostbite he never felt. It was like a road map to a sensation that doesn't exist. In the story, he claimed he felt emotions. He claimed he knew joy, love, sorrow, grief, loneliness. He was sure of it because of that last one. He was constantly lonely. No one wanted him around because he frightened people. At 34 years old, he had never had sex and had only kissed one person in his life. He remembers the way his lips felt that one time and how inside he felt something that seemed like fire. In that kiss, he could imagine what it might feel like to be burnt. What it might feel like to be warm. Or cold. It was as if this kiss had the power to awaken in him something he didn't even know existed. But it was just one kiss. And that was years ago. There was a picture of him with the story and looking at him I could see that he was waiting to be kissed again. When I read that story I wanted so badly to find him and kiss him. I wanted to open him up to the sharp edges of life. To something warm and dangerous. I called the newspaper and tracked down the writer. I made up a convincing story about being a long-lost relative and the writer gave me the man's phone number. I called. But the phone just rang and rang. I called for weeks until it seemed like he would never re-emerge. I eventually just gave up.

A few weeks later I saw another little blurb in the paper that I immediately understood. On the lower left corner of page A9 a headline read, "Man Who Doesn't Feel Pain Ends Life in Hotel Room." The article gave the pieced-together details of a night he spent with a prostitute. He was found dead, smiling, with lipstick on his face.

(*A drinks from his glass.*)

I hope I'm so lucky when it's my turn.

THIS IS HOW IT GOES
BY NEIL LABUTE

A threesome, who knew each other in high school, meet again after twelve years. Belinda has married Cody, an African-American former track star. The MAN *describes* HIMSELF *as being an "ex-lawyer, an ex-husband, and ex-military."* HE *has just left the couple to get a drink, but speaks to the audience.*

SCENE
A restaurant in a smallish town in the Midwest

TIME
Yesterday

MAN: Is it me, or does he seem a little pissed off? I totally get that vibe from him. Pissed right off about something. (*Beat.*) He didn't always used to be that way, not when I knew him, anyhow. Not that we were, like, tight or anything. Best buds. But I knew him enough . . . enough to say that much about him, and he never seemed so keyed up like this. I mean, maybe after his mom left, for a while there he was kinda . . . you know. How you get when that sort of thing happens. You're just cruising along and then, wham! Life gets, like, all shitty. Matter of minutes. . . . I think that's what happened to him. And, thing is, she'd do it about every other *month*. Plus, there's the whole race thing . . . not that he made a huge deal about it at school, but yeah, he pulled that card out a few times back then. Just once or twice a *day*! Nobody really called him on it, but it was completely obvious when he'd do it. School lunch line, picking teams for gym, when some girl or other wouldn't go out with him . . . like, *whenever* he needed some excuse, basically. We used to call it the ol' "Ace 'a Spades." I mean, not to his face, God no, you kidding? Cody was, well, you know . . . kinda fierce. Pretty serious when he wanted to be, so no. We'd say it when we were alone, just a few of the guys. Say, like, "Hey, Cody just whipped out the Ace 'a Spades." And that's when somebody'd say, one of my friends would . . . "Just gotta call a spade a spade." (*Smiles.*) We were only just joking, but it was pretty funny. At the time . . .

THREE DAYS OF RAIN

BY RICHARD GREENBERG

PIP, *the son of a famous architect who died when* HE *was very young, describes how his parents met.*

SCENE
New York City

TIME
Middle of the night

PIP: (*Solo.*) Hi. Hello. Okay: now me.

My name is Phillip O'Malley Wexler—well, Pip to those who've known me a little too long. My father, the architect Theodore Wexler, died of lung cancer at the age of 38, even though he was the only one of his generation who never smoked. I was 3 when it happened, so, of course, I forgot him instantly. My mother tried to make up for this by obsessively telling me stories about him, this kind of rolling epic that trailed me through life, but they, or *it*, ended up being mostly about her. Which was probably for the best.

Anyway, it went like this:

My mother, Maureen O'Malley back then, came to New York in the spring of '59. She was 20, her parents staked her to a year, and she arrived with a carefully thought out plan to be amazing at something. Well, the year went by without much happening and she was miserable because she was afraid she was going to have to leave New York and return, in disgrace, to Brooklyn.

Early one morning, after a night when she couldn't sleep at all, she started wandering around the city. It was raining, she had her umbrella, she sat in the rain under her umbrella on a bench in Washington Square Park, and felt sorry for herself. Then she saw my father for the first time.

"There he was," she told me, "this devastatingly handsome man" — that was an exaggeration, he looked like me — and he was obviously, miraculously, even *more* unhappy than she was. He was just thrashing through the rain, pacing and thrashing, until, all at once, he stopped and sank onto the bench beside her. But not because of her. He didn't realize she was there. He didn't have an umbrella so my mother shifted hers over to him.

"Despair," my mother told me, "can be attractive in a young person. Despair in a young person can be seductive."   .

Well, eventually she got tired of him not noticing the wonderful thing she was doing for him so she said, a little too loudly:

"Can I help you? May I be of help to you?"

Because he'd been crying.

And he jumped! Man, he *shrieked*!

But he stayed anyway, and they talked, and I was born, the end.

Okay. So, my mother had been telling me that story for about ten years before it occurred to me to ask: "Why was he crying? What was my father so upset about the first time he met you?" "I never knew," she said. He just told her he was fine, she took him to breakfast, they talked about nothing, and I guess she kind of gawked at him. And the more she gawked, I guess the happier he felt, because by the end of breakfast it was as if nothing had happened and they were laughing and my mother was in love and the worst day of her life had become the best day of her life.

When she first came to New York, my mother would stay up till dawn debating Abstract Expressionism and *Krapp's Last Tape*, and then she'd sneak out to a matinee of one of those plays you could never remember the plot of where the girl got caught in the rain and had to put on the man's bathrobe and they sort of did a little dance around each other and fell in love. And there wasn't even a single good joke, but my mother would walk out after and the city seemed dizzy with this absolutely random happiness, and that's how she met my father.

She's hardly ever home anymore. She travels from city to city.

I think she's looking for another park bench, and another wet guy. That's okay. I hope she finds him.

THREE DAYS OF RAIN
BY RICHARD GREENBERG

The son of a famous architect has returned to his late father's New York apartment after disappearing for a year. Not entirely stable, WALKER *relates his version of the past as* HE *tries to come to grips with the present.*

SCENE
WALKER*'s bed, in a somewhat dilapidated, spartanly furnished apartment located on a winding street in downtown Manhattan*

TIME
Middle of the night

WALKER: Meanwhile, back in the city. . . . Two nights of insomnia. In this room, in the dark . . . listening . . . soaking up the Stravinsky of it. . . . No end to the sounds in a city. . . . Something happens somewhere, makes a noise, the noise travels, charts the distance: The Story of a Moment.

God, I need to sleep! (HE *lets out a breath, takes in the room.*)

Yes. All right. Begin. (*Lights fill in.* WALKER *addresses us.*)

My name is Walker Janeway. I'm the son of Edmund Janeway, whose slightly premature death caused such a stir last year, I'm told.

As you're probably aware, my father, along with that tribe of acolytes who continue to people the firm of Wexler Janeway, designed all—yes, *all*—of the most famous buildings of the last thirty years. You've seen their pictures, you may have even visited a few. That Reform Synagogue in Idaho. The new library in Bruges. The crafts museum in Austin, that hospice I forget where, a vertical mall in Rhode Island that in square footage actually exceeds the *state* of Rhode Island.

Years and years and years ago, with his late partner, Theodore Wexler, my father also designed three or four buildings that truly *are* distinguished, chief among them: Janeway House.

I know you know that one.

Everyone's seen that one picture, *LIFE* magazine, April of '63, I think, where it looks lunar, I mean, like something carved from the moon, mirage-y—you remember that photo? It's beautiful, isn't it? It won some kind of non-Pulitzer Prize that year. People have sometimes declined my invitation to see the real place for fear of ruining the experience of the photograph.

Well. The real place, as it happens, is a private home out in the desirable part of Long Island. My grandparents commissioned it of my father, using all the money they had in the world, because, I guess, they loved him so much. Apparently, there was something there for a parent to love. Hard to imagine how they could tell, though, since he seldom actually spoke. Maybe he was lovable in a Chaplinesque way. Whatever, their faith paid off. The house is now deemed, by those who matter, to be one of the great private residences of the last half-century.

It's empty now.

My sister and I will inherit it today.

We'll be the only family present. Unless you count our friend, Pip, who is my late father's late partner's torpid son.

My mother would be with us, too, of course, but she's, um, like, well, she's sort of like Zelda Fitzgerald's less stable sister, so she can't be there. She's elsewhere, she's . . .

So, then, this is my story as I know it so far:

My father was more-or-less silent; my mother was more-or-less mad. They married because by 1960 they had reached a certain age and they were the last ones left in the room.

And then they had my sister who is somehow *entirely* sane.

And then they had me.

And my father became spectacularly successful, and his partner died shockingly young, and my mother grew increasingly mad, and my sister and I were there so we had to grow up.

VIA CRUCIS

BY ALBERT INNAURATO

JOHN *is 30 and in his first job, teaching basic playwriting to all comers and a survey course of the "Modern Drama." It's a big college, and they do lots of plays.* JOHN, *in pursuit of tenure (down the road some), has agreed to play a role in a fashionable play by a young lady, younger than* HE *is, who has gotten much acclaim and a Genius Grant.* HE *went to Yale School of Drama, so did she.*

SCENE
The stage, during a break in a frenzied rehearsal

TIME
Today

JOHN: God. I never thought going to the bathroom would be so painful. I have to run it out, it burns. And don't you smirk at me, it's not VD. Jesus, I wish this break would end. I bet they're all up in the office, drinking! They can't face this piece of shit any more than I can!! And it got a Genius Grant! This is the twenty-first century—it can't be because she's female any more, can it? Aren't they over that? And she's white, and not handicappable, and single and probably loved, and certainly whole, and she's got her fucking meal ticket written for the next forty years. I had to beg for this job, and it's only because Doc finally had a stroke at

89 that they needed me. Of all the sewage-strewn bad luck, to end up back here. I'd fled, goddamn it, I'd FLED!!!!!

Get away from me. I'm not going to run lines with you, her lines, God give her VD. I saw her and knew the enemy, she was in the class that came in my third year. She had this glow—some people smell of luck you know? One sniff, everybody who can write a check rushes to do it. Oh, Jesus, it still burns—do you fuckin' want to point out one goddamn line in this Sanctum Sanctorum of manure that *lives*. Look, I had this fat girl with bad skin in my fuckin' playwriting class. *She* had talent. Wrote this short play we read. Was about all these people—we thought—trying to get upwards somehow. It was a riddle of some kind. "OK, Sarah," I said, "what's the riddle?" "It's a glass jar full of fancy olives, and they're all trying to get picked. It's about you!" Gave me pause, and that's more than this minaret of manure does. I've got to pace some.

I had this revolutionary procedure at Yale. My mother stuck a pencil up my dick when I was 11. She said she was schizophrenic and a penis was a dangerous thing, intact. I'm not sure, but I think they patted her on the head and gave her an annuity. They put *me* in prison, they called it a home. Could have fooled Charles Manson. Left me with chronic urethral strictures. They stick a pipe up you, it's called a sound. They start rubber, then build up to steel—that's so you can pee again—for a while. But that just makes the strictures worse, because of the force and trauma. So they had this new operation. They cut you, you see—the area they work in is the size of a pencil point—they cut you, turn you inside out and give you a hole under your balls. You pee sitting down for six months. Then they try to remake you, so the stricture is absorbed, and you can piss again, like a man, like a horse! But one tiny slip—so I pee a lot and it burns and yes, I have to go again but I'm not giving in, and I'll never have children. (*Yells.*) Hey, director and older actors we need you on the stage!!!! Oh, where the fuck have they fled? Maybe they all hopped the train for fucking New Haven to try and get Genius Grants. Old codger genius grants! I'm sure they have them. If only I wasn't so fuckin' needy — for tenure, for a good stream, for some kind of success in life . . . if only . . .

(HE *thinks.*) "In Darkness Let Me Dwell." It's going through my head. It's a song by John Dowland. "Semper Dowland, semper dolens" — his motto. I'd like to keep writing plays, some of what I did was good. . . . But I feel obsolescent. We have movies now, we have 4,121 channels on your basic primitive TV, there's On Demand, there are DVDs — plays? Whatever fucking function the theater had way back when — gone!! (*Whistles.*) You know at Yale they have this program for critics — yes, they have to be taught to hate! I sat in on one of their seminars. They never talked about plays, old, new, weird — never! It was all movies. About the earliest movies, about thirties movies, about the auteur theory — a cliché nowadays in case you want to apply — about the irrelevance of narrative in the motion picture, about myth and the motion picture, about irony in the moving image, about the transcendence of animation. They took a poll one day of the greatest artistic achievement in the twentieth century. It was a foreign film about a donkey that keeps getting beaten for two hours. I was about to scream, "I am that donkey," when they started on the value of TV, especially subversive cartoons.

Oh God, I'm a eunuch and an anachronism: I believe there is a point to the live theater, to words as spoken, to the feeling that an actor is breathing right there, in space, in time, and can die or give birth, or even in some mysterious way, live for you — right there. I'm so ashamed, I haven't told anyone the surgeon slipped. Not my father, not the girls who hang around outside my classrooms. I want to grab someone in the street and shout, "Make me whole, please, please, make me whole." And now, now — I can't hold it any longer — I have to pee again. If they come back — ask them to wait for me. I can't afford to be difficult.

THE VIOLET HOUR
BY RICHARD GREENBERG

In this messy new publishing house, GIDGER *is the ageless "flunky" to young boss John Pace Seavering. They are both looking for some theatre tickets lost amidst the clutter. When speaking,* GIDGER*'s manner is somewhat extravagant.*

SCENE
John Pace Seavering's office and its anteroom in a Manhattan tower

TIME
April 1919. Early afternoon to early evening.

GIDGER: Every night it's the same thing. I return home to my garret after my day of . . . *this* . . . and I ask him, dutifully, Would you like to be walked?

And INVARIABLY he replies: Yes, I would like very much to be walked.

Never ONCE does he inquire as to whether I really FEEL like walking him. Never ONCE has he picked up on my mood.

Would you like to be walked?

Yes, I would like very much to be walked.

Garish mandibles dripping leash.

Tail swishing like a bobbin, like a SHUTtlecock, the long-sought machine of perpetual motion.

Would you like to be walked?

Yes, I would like very much to be walked.

Would you like to be fed?

Yes, I would like very much to be fed.

Well, maybe I DON'T FEEL LIKE IT!

Maybe I need a DRINK and a FOOT RUB!

Nono!

Would you like to be walked?

Yes, I would like very much to be walked.

Would you like to be fed?

Yes, I would like very much to b —

A DOG'S LIFE? You know who leads a dog's life?

A DOG'S MASTER.

I'm going to have him killed.

[JOHN: You're not.

GIDGER: I'm seriously considering it.

JOHN: You wouldn't kill—What's his name?]

GIDGER: Sir Lancelot. But sometimes I call him Lance and sometimes
I call him Sir. Sometimes I call him Lancie, sometimes I call
him La. Sometimes I call him Celot, sometimes I call him Slut.
Sometimes I call him Lut sometimes I call him Sla sometimes I
call him Ut. With each new name, I HOPE to call forth some as
yet undiscovered and admirable aspect of his personality.

(*Shakes his head sharply, a definite punctuation.*)

[JOHN: (*Mildly.*)You're not going to kill your puppy.

GIDGER: (*The anguish of the powerless.*) Can't I even kill my *dog?*

JOHN: No.]

GIDGER: What do I *have?*

I live in *Queens!*

THE VIOLET HOUR
BY RICHARD GREENBERG

At 25, JOHN PACE SEAVERING *is starting a publishing house, but can't decide what to publish. When a mysterious machine arrives in the office which provides the future of the protagonists,* JOHN *is confused about his existence, and also about Rosamund Plinth, who left the office threatening suicide. Here* HE *speaks of a conversation* HE *had "yesterday."*

SCENE
JOHN PACE SEAVERING'*s office and its anteroom in a Manhattan tower*

TIME
April 1919. Early afternoon to early evening.

JOHN: It wasn't much of a conversation.

But he transcribed every word.

Why did he take it all down? Why are we all such recordists?

Don't we know that . . . ?

Everyone's taking everything down as if it's historical, as if it's
historic.

As if it's witty or sums up the Times.

All of us confident, all of us aquiver with self-importance. I've read
things I said three weeks ago, and things I said three years ago,
and things that were said back to me. And things that were not
said quite that way, and things that were said back but not quite
so well.

Gidger?

(*Beat.*)

We all sound alike.

I thought we were each unique.

I held our distinctions in such high regard.

I thought our nuances were essential.

I can't hear them anymore.

When I read them . . . I don't hear them.

We all sound the same.

(*Beat.*)

We sound like the past.

Even you, Gidger—even back when you seemed the opposite of everything—you were just . . . a different tempo in the same signature—I don't want to think about it.

(HE *crosses to the window.*)

On the street there's a woman standing in front of a shop window. Her chin is propped on her finger. She's trying to decide whether to buy a dress.

Across the street from her—she doesn't see this—a man is taking her photograph.

I know what the photograph will look like. All shades of gray and the light bunching behind her, that ghost look.

This all happened *ages* ago.

Look at us, Gidger—we're *peri*od.

These aren't clothes we're wearing—they're costumes.

(*The phone rings.* JOHN *grabs it.*)

Yes?

Oh . . . oh, thank you, yes, I'm very grateful to you . . .

Oh, she hasn't . . .

Yes, please, I would so appreciate it.

Yes, thank you very much.

(He *hangs up.*)

The concierge at Miss Plinth's building . . . she hasn't appeared, but he heard the note of concern in my voice . . . and . . .

People were so considerate back when we lived.

THE VOYAGE OF THE CARCASS
BY DAN O'BRIEN

BILL, *a disillusioned actor in his early 30s, laments his failed career and the state of the theatre, but is really lashing out at his wife, Helen, and best friend, whom* HE *suspects are having an affair.*

SCENE
A small theatre in the middle of nowhere

TIME
Today

[HELEN: What are you talking about, Bill?]

BILL: I'm talking about the state of American Theatre! A fucking corpse, that's what it is! A fucking cadaver! Nobody cares — nobody fucking cares anymore!

[HELEN: That's right: nobody cares, so shut up —]

BILL: Shakespeare totally sucks! — Who decided he was good? Hm? A bunch of high school English teachers who figured out that *Julius Caesar* was cheaper than horse tranquilizers? Things would be so much easier if I were a woman . . .

[HELEN: Bill —]

BILL: No, wait: if I were a black, quadriplegic lesbian clown . . . I would have so much more grant money!

[HELEN: You'd never get to Broadway.]

BILL: — Fuck Broadway! — And off-Broadway. And off-off-off-Broadway. And the "downtown theatre scene." And "regional theatre." And "festivals," and "workshops." And theatre about "thorny social issues." Fuck dramas. And comedies — fuck revivals; above all fuck revivals! Of musicals! Fuck all musicals. And plays based on literature in the public domain. — Fuck the public domain! Fuck the public! — No, I love my public, wherever they may be: fuck the proletariat. Fuck critics, speaking of commie pinko bastards. Fuck *The New York Fucking Times* and *The Star-Fucking-Ledger*. Fuck old people. And their fucking little crackling candies. Fuck "subscribers." Fuck suburban housewives from New Jersey and their narcoleptic banker-husbands. — I fucking hate New Jersey so fucking much! — Fuck tourists from Idaho, or Iowa, whichever, doesn't matter. Fuck Disney, of course. Fuck old people, again, one more time. And kids fresh from Juilliard, or NYU, or Brown. Fuck hipsters from Williamsburg. And as much as it pains me to say this because some of my best friends are members but: fuck the gay mafia. And lesbians, if they even have a mafia. Do they? They should. Fuck "Yalies." Fuck trust-fund babies. Fuck actors and writers of all stripes — and mimes. And clowns. Fuck me. Above all fuck me. Above all you must all go ahead and fuck me so hard.

WE HAD A VERY GOOD TIME

BY DAVID AUBURN

DIMA, *a self-appointed tour guide, is telling Nicole, an American woman desparate for adventure, and determined to explore the native culture, about the revolution that occurred ten years earlier. His story may or may not be accurate, but* DIMA*'s aim is to seduce Nicole.*

SCENE
An unnamed Eastern country

TIME
The present

DIMA: Some people on the barricades on the avenue realized what was going on. They ran over here, a dozen of them. The tanks were just turning the corner into this plaza. It was midnight, very dark, August first, a hot night. No moon; the demonstrators carried flashlights. They didn't have weapons. A couple had Molotov cocktails but these are useless unless the tanks are open and besides these are our people driving the tanks. A couple dozen more people had arrived: as many as could leave the barricade on the avenue. They lay down on the pavement. Stretched out — spread their arms and legs wide: there were just enough people to do this and reach all the way across the plaza with their fingertips touching. They were lying there in the path of the tanks. Staring straight up at the sky: no moon, no stars, cloudy night. It was humid. The tanks had to stop. That was the idea — that the boys driving the tanks would not drive over their brothers, cousins, classmates, their girlfriends in the street. The tanks stopped. For a minute no one knew what to do. Everyone was lying there. The pavement was very uncomfortable. Then one of the protesters stood up. He shouted at the tanks. "Soldiers! Remember that you have taken an oath to your country. Your weapons cannot be turned against the people! Clouds of terror and dictatorship are gathering over us but this night will not be eternal and our long-suffering people will find freedom once again, and forever. Soldiers! I believe at this fateful hour you will make the right decision. The honor of our country will not be covered with the blood of the people. Join us." Everyone was waiting. Then the top of one tank opened and a soldier popped his head out. He looked very small. He had a rifle and he threw it to the pavement. Everyone leaped up. Everyone cheered. The other tanks opened. The soldiers poured out of the hatches. They threw away their guns. They were dancing on top of the tanks. Girls climbed up on the tanks and kissed the soldiers. We swarmed around the tanks. One soldier had a tape deck. He turned it on full blast. The Beatles singing "Twist and Shout." Everyone was dancing, kissing, crying. It happened right here.

WTC VIEW

BY BRIAN SLOAN

ALEX *is a 27-year-old Wall Street guy from Goldman Sachs, dressed for the corporate scene.* HE *has come to look at a room Eric is trying to rent out. In their interview Eric's remarks elicit* ALEX's *painful tale of escaping from Tower One.*

SCENE
An apartment in SoHo

TIME
The last week of September 2001

ALEX: I had an early meeting that morning to go over some new bonds. The meeting ended around quarter of nine and —

[ERIC: That's right when the — how'd you get out?]

ALEX: I was in the Sky Lobby and everyone was getting off the elevators, going to work. So I got in an empty elevator by myself and hit the lobby button. And I'm just standing there, whistling and looking at my feet . . . you know, elevator stuff. Then suddenly the whole thing comes to a stop and there's this huge whoosh of air, then a low rumbling sound. And the lights and everything flicker off for a minute but then come back on. I tried to open the doors but they were stuck. And then I heard some voices coming from the speaker but it was all jumbled. Then there was another rumbling sound, not as big. After that I was beginning to think this is probably pretty serious but still I didn't know what was going on. A voice comes on the speaker that I can finally understand and says there's a fire and that someone's coming to get me. So I just stand there waiting. So I wait and wait and wait. No one comes. All I can see is this sliver of dusty light through the doors and I think maybe I should try to open them again. So I did and they opened. Just like that. I couldn't believe it, but all that time I was in the lobby. On the ground floor. So I walk out and look around and all the windows are smashed and there's all this smoke but there are no people. I mean *no one* is around. So I walk out to the plaza and there is just—all this . . . luggage. Suitcases that are open and garment bags and business clothes and shoes. . . so many pairs of shoes. Then I hear this huge thump behind me—almost like a mini-explosion. And about twenty feet away is what I guess is a body . . . not 'cause it looks like one. But because of all the blood. So I look up and see two more coming down, holding up tablecloths as these makeshift parachutes that would work for a few seconds and then . . . don't. At that point I knew I should run but with all this carnage and things falling I didn't know where to go. I froze. Then, outta nowhere, I feel something on my wrist—something that's burning hot. I think I'm on fire for a minute, that some piece of something's hit me, but I turn around and there's this huge fireman grabbing me by the wrist and he starts running, dragging me behind him. I tried to slow down and turn around and see exactly what the hell's going on, but the fireman yells, "Don't turn around." And hearing that . . . I just get shivers all over my body. So we're just booking—down Fulton, over to West Street. Even though we're running, I feel cold all of a sudden. The only part of my body that feels warm is my wrist where he's holding me, and it's really starting to hurt. Finally, we get to the river where all these fireboats are parked and I hear this enormous crack, like a clap of thunder. I turn around to see it falling—coming down into this insane cloud that starts barreling toward us. The fireman just about throws me on a fireboat but the cloud stops before it gets to us. So I'm sitting on the boat and just shaking . . . I'm so cold. And a nurse comes up to me, staring at me, and asks if I'm hurt and I look at my pants and there's all this blood but it's not mine—it's from the plaza. So she checks me out and I'm not hurt at all. Not a scratch. The only thing I had was this big bruise on my wrist from the fireman. From his grip. That's all.

PART TWO

THE EXTENDED MONOLOGUE

THE ANNIVERSARY

BY SPALDING GRAY

On one of the happiest days of the year, SPALDING GRAY *encounters mortality and the existential nature of life.*

SCENE
A table and chair, a glass of water

TIME
2000

SPALDING: On the morning of January 12, 2000, I woke with the usual anxious feeling caused by the lingering bottom-line memory that one day, never to be known by me until I'm there, that I, as I have come to know myself, will disappear forever, and ever, and forever, amen. End of story.

Kathie tried to cheer me up by reminding me that today was our tenth anniversary. That we met in Rochester ten years ago.

I don't think Kathie and I made love or had sex that morning because Theo was sleeping with us, and that always diffuses any chance for a pure, flat-out erotic event.

But on this day, January 12, 2000, I do remember the following. I remember Theo not eating his cereal. Kathie had gone to work, and I was taking care of him. I remember he quickly got bored of the TV, and wanted to play the piano with me. We did that for a while, improvising in our own way.

Then he wanted to play the Mummy with me. He had recently seen the video *The Mummy* a number of times and was most caught up by the scene in which the central character is being punished for his transgressions with the pharaoh's wife. He is being punished by being placed in a coffin and then wrapped alive like a mummy. Then the soulless pharaoh's guards turn over this large jar filled with these horrific, swarming black beetles that Theo kept referring to as "the Bees."

And these black beetles swarmed toward this poor man's head and most likely devour his living brain in a matter of seconds.

And this is what my 3-year-old Theo is most interested in having me help him reenact. And I get to be the Mummy.

"Get in the box, Daddy, get in the box," he says.

And I lie down on the floor and pretend to be the Mummy.

For a moment it feels so good to be lying so still and quiet. And then Theo releases "the Bees." And I start screaming, to his delight.

Theo and I meet Kathie at 11:30 AM and walk over to a nursing home on the Lower East Side. It is at this nursing home that Theo's godmother Freya has been vegetating for over a year and a half from a series of strokes she had while summering in Africa.

It is an unthinkable situation that has to be thought about. Particularly by her daughter, who does not, for so many apparent reasons, does not execute her mother's living will. How could she? Her mother talks and cries and still has a sense of humor. And she is only my age. And I am only hers.

The first time I brought Theo to see her in that nursing home his whole being went into a kind of electrified alert. The minute he entered he was all bug-eyed and looking every which way. What is this?

This time Theo is calmer. And Freya is less aware of him. She can't see, and can hardly understand how she has come to be wherever it is—she is not sure. She is in an obviously horrific bardo state. Somewhere in between living and dying. It's as if she comes alive only for visitors and then returns to some limbo state where time does not exist.

When we ask her what she thinks about she says, "Juice." She also dreams about juice. She loves to drink juice. I apologize for not bringing some. I will do it next time, I tell her.

We don't stay long. We promise to return soon.

On the way out, Kathie says, "It's awful. She doesn't know what to do. She doesn't know what to feel. She doesn't deserve this. What did she do to deserve this?"

I am amazed that Kathie still seems to believe in some intrinsic justice system. Some absolute, hierarchical reward program. And at that moment I wondered if she too believed in fate.

On the way to the nursing home, Kathie had told me that she had just found out that our Sag Harbor neighbor Carlos was in St. Vincent's Hospital with pneumonia. He had been in there for over a week and we hadn't gotten the message on our answering machine. The doctors didn't expect him to live. Carlos was Theo's oldest buddy, and Theo was Carlos's youngest friend. We had to go right away.

When we got there we met Carlos's wife, Marie, and their daughter and her husband. They'd all been pretty much camping out at the hospital for the past week.

Carlos's wife, Marie, who is in her early 70s, was her old chatty self and very up. She was sure that Carlos was going to pull through even though the doctors only gave him a one percent chance. Marie was so enthusiastic about the emergency room and all the nurses that she wanted to give me her own tour right away, starting with the four-hundred-pound Egyptian who was also lying in bed with pneumonia.

She told me how it took six men to carry him in. I peeked in at him, or rather at the massive bulk of bedding I took to be him. A small woman I took to be his wife was kneeling and praying over his giant body.

When I at last came to Carlos, with all those tubes coming out of him, I really didn't know what to say, but I felt I had to say something. Marie told me he was not conscious, but I thought he might still be able to hear me. I said, "Hi, Carlos. It's Spalding. I hope you get better soon."

I wish I had had a new joke to tell him, but I didn't. I don't remember any jokes, except for the one Carlos told me. The one that goes, "A skeleton walked into a bar, and ordered a glass of beer and a mop."

Outside in the waiting room, Marie told me that there were people all over the world praying for Carlos. She also told me that if I needed any kindling to start my fire at home, to look in their driveway because Carlos had left a pile of sticks there for me. Was that where his life had stopped?

Going down on the elevator with Kathie and Theo, I thought, Why not pray for Carlos? It might be better than just standing here waiting for the elevator to reach the first floor. I didn't know how to pray or who to pray to, so I just did the first thing that came to mind. I imagined myself standing at the end of Carlos's bed. I visualized a warm ball of energy at the base of my spine. It looked like a little sun. Then I let it rise up my spine and burst out the top of my head. It burst out like a volcano of multicolored confetti, and it sprayed up and out and settled on Carlos like a colorful electric snow. Like a 60s poster, I thought, and at the same time I wondered why I hadn't prayed for my dad when he was dying in the hospital.

Outside, on the street, Kathie asked me if I had cried when I saw Carlos. "No," I said, "did you?" "Yes," she said, "I couldn't help it."

On the sidewalk outside St. Vincent's, Kathie suggested that I take Theo to ride on the carousel in Central Park. "What a great idea," I said. "I am so glad you thought of that."

Theo and I took a cab to Fifty-ninth Street and Sixth Avenue. I couldn't stand to look out the window at the city, so I watched Theo watching the city. I never took my eyes off him for the whole trip.

Once we got to the park, Theo got very involved with all the natural rock outcroppings. I had never realized how real they were until I saw him playing on them. Before this day they had always seemed somewhat artificial in my mind. I hadn't realized how big they were and how many there were between Fifty-ninth Street and the carousel.

Theo seemed to feel no need to get to the merry-go-round. He was happy just climbing on the rocks. But I, who thought I really wanted to make it to the carousel before it closed, kept saying, "C'mon, Theo, don't you want to ride on the horsies?"

We arrived at the carousel just a few minutes before it was to close. There was a man already slamming down some of the sliding metal doors. Oh, what a violent sound.

We were the only ones on the merry-go-round and it was going very fast. Theo was on an outside horse, and I was on the horse just in from him. I looked over at Theo going up and down to the music and I saw that he was very, very happy. He was purely, utterly, very happy. There was no room for anything else but the happiness that filled him.

I don't remember who did it first, but . . . no, it was me . . . or was it I? Anyway, I let out with a yell that was sort of half performed and half spontaneously real. In other words, I was quite aware of it coming out of me and how it sounded. And I do know that it was my yell that triggered Theo, and he just lifted his head back and let out with this yelping, joyful cry. It was like out of a movie, only better. His cry just grabbed the whole day by the feet, by the short hairs, and gathered it up. It was pure celebration. It was unadulterated happiness.

That one ride was enough for both of us, and anyway it was clear they were closing the carousel down. Then, on my way out, Theo spotted "the treats." There was a little display of gum and candy at convenient child level, right on our way out. Theo seemed to know exactly what he wanted. It was what they call a "ring pop." A sort of candy pacifier. A plastic ring with a giant, glassy, ruby-red candy shaped like a Walt Disney diamond.

I picked up the ring pop and looked around but didn't see anyone handy to pay. So I just dropped it into my pocket. I'd never done anything like that before, or at least not often, and I didn't give it a second thought.

As we were leaving, the man closing the metal doors turned and said, "What about that candy, mister?" I was taken completely by surprise. "Oh this?" I said, pulling out the ring pop from my pocket. "What do I owe you?"

"That's fifty cents."

Then he suddenly changed his mind and said, "No, give it back. We are closed here now."

I watched Theo watch me give the ring pop back to the man. Theo was incredulous, but at the same time seemed confused and intimidated by the power of the situation. What was wrong, he wondered, more than he needed that candy.

"Why, Dad? Why the guy say that?"

"None of us want you to eat so much candy, Theo," I said as I walked briskly up the path, pulling Theo by the hand. Behind us, the carousel man was making a fist with his hand and yelling after us, "Your son is going to end up in prison one day!"

At the top of the hill, just beyond the carousel, I could see the rows of American elms, catching the last of the day's light. They were all dark and twisting and casting incredible shadows on the green lawn. Should the grass be this green in January? I wondered as I sat down with Theo to gaze at my favorite place in Central Park. These trees, these trees, these beautiful trees.

As soon as we sat down, Theo asked for his bottle, and I pulled it out of my pocket and gave it to him. Then he leaned his head against my body while he sucked. While he drank.

On the way to the subway, every time I saw a cop, I saw the headlines:

MONOLOGUIST AND 3-YEAR-OLD SON CAUGHT RED-HANDED — TALK YOUR WAY OUT OF THIS ONE, MR. SPALDING.

Theo and I took the A train home. On the subway I tried thinking about the words "fate," "necessity" and "chance." I kept trying to put "necessity" and "sacred" together. I thought also about how I could not imagine living without my children, and how I would either have to die or learn to live without them. I thought about my mother and how she couldn't live without us, and how she took the more extreme way out. I thought about how none of this day would have been had I not gone alone to P.S. 122 to see the avant-garde drama that fateful night in November of 1989, where, while watching Frank Maya perform, I was tapped on the shoulder by Larry Champoux, who just happened to be Kathie Russo's boss at the Pyramid Arts Center in Rochester, New York.

"How would you like to come up and perform your stuff at our space?" he asked me.

"Sure, why not?" I said. "Here's my phone number — give me a call."

And he did.

And I went.

And Kathie Russo picked me up at the airport.

AUNT PITTI-PAT
IN THE TOWER
BY DAVID SIMPATICO

After witnessing the towers collapse on 9/11 and all that has ensued, an openly gay man channels his inner AUNT PITTI-PAT, *Scarlett O'Hara's hysterical aunt in* Gone with the Wind, *to confront a post-modern world. (Dedicated to the memory of Francis Riccardelli.)*

SCENE
A stage

TIME
The present

(*A* MAN *enters, carrying a section of the* New York Times.)

AUNT PITTI-PAT: "*Scarlett, the Yankees are comin', the Yankees are comin', I've got to get out of Atlanta before they burn it to the ground, those nasty Yankee devils. Oh Scarlett, I tell you I don't know what to do, I don't know what to do, I simply do not know what to do—where are my smelling salts?*"

Atlanta fell all over again in eight seconds. Floor after floor upon floor after floor of steel and concrete and desks and chairs and memos and pictures of the kids slamming down one upon the other upon the next upon ton after ton after ton on top of the heads of the old ladies and MBAs and Billy in the Grounds department picking the onion off of his bagel and all the mailroom clerks and CEOs — 110 floors of life slamming down onto their heads just one floor below and flattening them, exploding them, smashing their cells apart like overripe tomatoes caught beneath a mile-high slab of smooth concrete.

In eight tiny seconds Frannie Riccardelli, who was in charge of all vertical movement in both towers, who ran back into the building trying to save the people caught in the elevator cars who had already died behind the closed doors, Frannie Riccardelli with the bad breath and big smile who was my friend since the third week of the fourth grade and asked me to be his Holy Roman Sponsor even though he was two days older than me, Frannie Riccardelli who had five kids and a wonderful wife and a huge smile. Frannie Riccardelli who couldn't be buried because there was nothing left to bury.

His teeth and eyes and tongue and fingers and ass and blood and bad breath blown to the winds, in a half a heartbeat blown apart unable to resist the mile of concrete crushing down upon his head. His big toothy smile shattered forever except for the memories and videotapes his wife will play for his five fatherless children.

Frannie Riccardelli blown apart while I watched from my fabulous thank you God Greenwich Village loft on the ninth floor facing south with the spectacular three-quarter views drinking coffee on my terrace facing south and loving the view, MY view with the clear blue sky and the smell of morning and not thinking about that plane until it explodes the perfect view from my terrace in the blink of an eye.

On the phone screaming crying shaking watching Atlanta fall in eight seconds, the only thought left in my head "how many people did I just watch die?", screaming in my beautiful loft with the wraparound view.

Walking around staggering stunned in the sudden quarantine of Fourteenth Street roped off filled with speeding tanks and militia and empty ambulances and tired firemen pulling their feet behind them while the rest of us give a standing ovation on the curb and Virginia the sexy Puerto Rican grandmother who cleans my apartment in the fluorescent green stretch-pants every other week runs out with water and throws her arms around some hunky Irishman covered in dust and death, throws her arms around him and kisses him, MY HERO MY HERO.

Walking around in the gathering dust, the dust in the gentle change of wind, dust and asbestos and concrete and something else floating up from the Financial District, a scent we all recognize in our guts, something sickly, something more than dust mixed in with the smoke and concrete.

Walking around the silent Village surrounded by thousands of smiling faces, Xeroxed in black and white and color, smiling faces of the Recently Lost plastered like wallpaper onto the A&P and Ray's Original Pizza, smiling husbands and sons and sisters and lovers and daughters and cousins and fathers and mothers and Frannie Riccardelli, all lost and waiting to be found, in some hospital probably, but the hospitals are sad and empty and waiting for someone, anyone to come in — smiling faces blown apart all lost until we breathe them in through our nostrils and down into our lungs. And then we spit them up, gagging.

I can't sleep anymore. All I want to do is get a gun and kill someone. I mean that in the good way.

Oh, the *Times*, the *Times*. I hate the *Times*, thank God for the *Times*. Every day the *Times* picks through the rubble with far greater success than all the rescue workers combined, picking through the smashed remains for the smiling faces, for the lives lost, finds them and reduces them to a smiling face and a headline. "Bronco Busting Boy Scout," "Loving Son and Broker." Today, they found Frannie Riccardelli, "Planner of Family Fun."

They left a lot out. They left out how Frannie and I used to wait until the sun went down in my backyard and catch lightning bugs, how we used to think we could decode their little blinking language and understand them, caught forever in the eternal embrace of a pickle jar.

Oh, Scarlett, Melanie, where in heavens is my sense of humor, I need my sense of—oh, here it is.

(*Looking in the newspaper.*) Why look, Katie Couric is getting an eighty-million-dollar raise, and I can't find my Metrocard. Katie stayed up forty-eight hours straight. So did her hairdresser. How much did he get?

Perhaps I'd feel more secure if I read the full story, and not just the headlines on the way to the subway.

How do I prepare for BioTerrorist attacks? How much Vicks Vaporub will I *really* need?

I thought I was lucky because I got through AIDS in one piece, but now I have to worry about Dirty Bombs in Times Square, just when my career is taking off. Everyone's a critic.

I bought a cell phone when we started bombing Kuwait, I mean Afghanistan.

Personally, I liked the theme music for the Gulf War better.

The night I became one with my Pitti-Pat Within—you remember Pitti-Pat, Scarlett O'Hara's hysterical, snuff-swilling paranoic aunt with the sausage curls—anyway, I remember sitting in front of my television when the new kid on the block interrupted all programming, and stood in front of our American Flag, and said, Okay, come on now everybody, I won the election, that's all there is to it, let's eat. He interrupted all Friday night programming, including *Buffy*. And I thought for sure there would be a riot in the streets, I mean when was the last time we had our very own coup d'etat?

I was like a bird trapped inside a closet, bouncing off walls, flapping for cover, grasping at headlines or snippets or sound bites for some refuge from my fluttering paranoia and the revolution going on outside my door—*Atlanta is burning, where are my smelling salts?*

But there was no revolution. No reaction. No crowds breaking glass and stealing jeans and torching cars. Nothing.

And don't you know that Good Ol' Boy got just what he wanted, like a spoiled little rich kid entitled to something he wants simply because he wants it. Daddy's little boy with dime-store eyes. Daddy's little boy. I didn't vote for him. I'd fuck him, but I wouldn't vote for him.

I remember thinking when we invaded Kuwait, I don't even like those people. They'd kill me just because of who I choose to sleep with. Like I said, everyone's a critic.

I guess someone somewhere must think that this whole thing was a good idea. I wish I could understand that, I truly do. Like David and Goliath. I mean David got tired of hiding in his stinking little caves while the Giant stomped around the villages, tired of watching his children play hopscotch with land mines and having his tongue ripped out and fingers cut off and vanishing with muffled screams into the night while the Giant gives a helping hand and blind eye to the loss of lives and fingers and tongues and gouged eye sockets, supporting regimes and training fanatics who run riot until they bump into David practicing his aim, David who finally pokes his brown little head out of the cave and hits a goddamn bullseye.

Atlanta is burning. The sky is falling. Where are my smelling salts?

Frannie Riccardelli. Planner of Family Fun.

All that fire, burning, Atlanta, Afghanistan, Wall Street, Kuwait. They all look the same. Those poor little children hiding in the hills, in the caves. Under desks. Running down the fire stairs. Roasting, trapped in elevators ninety-four stories high. Heroes sacrificing their lives smashed under concrete as they try to save the dead. They all look the same.

I shouldn't think too much. Stick to the headlines. Because otherwise I start to think too much.

I start to think too much about *why Atlanta is burning.* And why David hates Goliath. And why Kuwait and Afghanistan sound the same. And why it all seems to be about the deed to the Holy Land and stepping into five-thousand-year-old shit and the millennium hanging over our heads like the sword of Damocles with a nuclear warhead and the Second Coming and Golden Parachutes and the Battle of Armageddon and Economic Globalization and the fall of Enron and Oil Concerns in the Middle East and Dick Cheney on the Board and will the real AntiChrist please stand up with the sky falling down upon our heads and the world changing forever in eight seconds and Frannie Riccardelli's bad breath.

(HE *picks up an empty pickle jar.*) I remember the night the wind changed, the air was filled with concrete and dust and death, I ran inside and found an old pickle jar. I took the jar out on my terrace, into the cloud of air swirling with the souls of the dead. I opened the jar and caught the air, like lightning bugs. I scooped as much air as the jar could hold, all the dust and death and pain and breath and hopes and dreams floating in the dusk. Scooped them into the jar so I could always have them. So I could always remember.

(HE *unscrews the jar, puts his face in it and breathes in deeply.*) The Tarot Card for Change is the Tower. Bolts of lightning smash a High Tower, which falls to the ground in a million pieces.

The Tarot Card for Change is the Tower. It brings a moment of quick and explosive insight, allowing us to see through the hidden.

The Tarot Card for Change is the Tower. When the dust has settled, it ushers in a new age. An age of illumination. And healing.

Smelling salts. They clear the head. They make you think.

THE COST OF LIVING
BY BRAD SCHREIBER

At 17, YOUNG MAN *recalls his first lesson in economics and labor negotiations, while lamenting the fact that the only constant in life is, in fact, change.*

SCENE
A stage

TIME
The present

YOUNG MAN: There's something going on . . . that's frightening me. It's not a conspiracy. It's not a plot. It's not just aimed at me. It's affecting everyone. But nobody has noticed it . . . except me. What am I talking about? I'll tell you. Just don't mention where you heard it.

(*Pause.*)

Change.

(*Insistent.*)

Change!

(*Quickly.*)

Everything is changing around us so fast that we have no reference points any more. That's what I'm talking about.

(*Unsure.*)

Well, perhaps I should elaborate. I'm not talking about suitcase bombs or artificial intelligence or smokeless ashtrays. That's scientific advancement. I'm not talking about animals becoming extinct, soil erosion or tsunamis. That's just Mother Nature. And I'm not talking about the coins in your purse or pocket because that's just . . .

(*Quickly.*)

. . . well, change, but it's not the kind of change I'm talking about, although it has something to do with it but . . .

(*Pause.*)

It's the constant change of traditions. The destruction of established norms, the shattering of the few expectations we still have left to hold onto.

(*Frustrated.*)

I suppose you want an example.

(He *paces, thinking. Stops.*)

All right. Here it is. You can't get a good candy bar in this country for under a dollar any more. It's this willful, negligent and unnecessary increase in the price of services and products that were at a standard price so long, they became part of the foundation of the American way of life!

(*Catches his breath. Smugly.*)

You're starting to follow me, aren't you? This didn't all start with the death of cheap candy. No way! Where *did* it start? Nobody knows. Because I'm the only one who's noticed it so far and I'm only 17 years old. This has probably been going on since man first traded polished stones for pieces of cooked dinosaur meat. But I can tell you when I first discovered this phenomenon.

(*Happily reminiscent.*)

As a boy, my family and I used to go to a place called the Four G's Restaurant for dinner. They had the best steaks in town. You got a thick, juicy cut of steak, a big baked potato with gobs of butter and sour cream and nice dinner salad with lots of different vegetables in it for $5.99. We went there once a week. The quality was uniform. The price was right. It became, like, a tradition.

(*Ominously.*)

And then, one terrible night, we arrived at Four G's only to read a sign in the window with three of the most terrifying words I've ever read together.

(*Mimes reading, slowly.*)

"Under . . . New . . . Management."

(He *walks toward an imaginary restaurant, staring at it, stunned.*)

What was wrong with the old management? They did good business. The place had plenty of customers. We were regulars. The

owner knew us by name. He was a great guy, Mister, uh, Mister. . . .
I can't remember his name right now, but anyway!

(HE *mimes walking inside the restaurant and sits.*)

We walked inside cautiously. Same plastic, red and white gingham
tablecloths. Same paintings of old sailing ships on the walls. Our
waitress was even the same. She handed us menus. Without even
looking, we order the usual. The waitress wrote down our order
and left.

(HE *mimes opening the menu.*)

Ten dollars and ninety-nine cents? We made tense small talk,
waiting for our food, fearing our food. And then it came.

(*Horrified.*)

Tough, dark wedges of meat, brimming with fat. A potato barely
the size of a golf ball. And a dinner salad that consisted of lots of
lettuce topped with one single cherry tomato.

(*Sadly philosophical.*)

My childhood died right there, that night. If the comfort of
my family's weekly dinner at Four G's could be taken away that
quickly, that pointlessly, then what tradition was safe? Soon
after that, I found out everything was up for grabs. The Big
Hunk candy bar I bought shrank into a little chunk. There were
suddenly fewer baseball cards in a pack and they cost more and
to try and make up for it, they gave you a thin, dried-up wafer
of gum, that crumbled like old parchment when you chewed
it.

(*Angrily.*)

I mean, my God, I was just a little kid and my world was systematically degraded and devalued.

(*Remembering.*)

I'm sure it was tough on my parents, too. But they were adults, used to the world of mortgages, down payments and short-term loans. All I knew was five dollars a week allowance, cash and carry.

(*Deep parental voice.*)

"Make it last!"

(*Normal voice.*)

My folks told me each week. But how was I supposed to stretch my shopping dollar when prices were multiplying like a hyperactive amoeba? I'll tell you, I was getting an education in economics that would put the Harvard Business School to shame.

(*Excitedly.*)

But I came up with a solution. Get more money! I went to management . . .

(*Sotto voce.*)

. . . my parents.

(*Normal voice.*)

And told them that labor . . .

(*Sotto voce.*)

. . . that's me . . .

(*Normal voice.*)

. . . was in need of a cost-of-living increase. Management took a hard line, claiming I hadn't fulfilled one clause in our oral agreement, specifically, washing the dishes every Tuesday. I suggested amending the current contract, bringing labor's salary up to the industry standard, which, according to my friend Jackie Heggemann was at least seven dollars a week. Management said, "No." I said, "What's your counteroffer?" They said,

(*Parental voice.*)

"we're not making a counteroffer."

(He *backs up, as if being threatened.*)

Management still didn't give an inch, although they did raise their voices. I was getting desperate. I tried $5.25 a week. Nothing. Five ten? Forget it. How about just deleting the clause concerning dishwashing?

(He *pathetically shakes his head no.*)

Management had me begging and pleading and they loved every minute of it. My back was to the living-room wall. I summoned my courage and informed them that if they remained unwilling to renegotiate the contract, labor would have no other alternative than to go on strike.

(He *smugly stands his ground.*)

That got them. They carefully sized me up, trying to determine if I'd go through with the strike threat.

(*Intensely.*)

The male half of management leaned forward, blew a puff of pipe smoke at me, and reminded me that if I struck, I could kiss goodbye my extensive benefits package, which included food, clothing and shelter. The female half of management . . .

(*Shouting.*)

SCREAMED THAT THOSE EMPLOYEE BENEFITS IN-CLUDED CLEANING, COOKING, SEWING, HEALTH CARE, TRANSPORTATION, EDUCATION AND MISCEL-LANEOUS EXPENSE ITEMS, LIKE MY TEN-SPEED BIKE AND BASEBALL GLOVE!

(*Reasonably.*)

I thought to myself, they've got a point. But my pride was at stake here, too. In an eleventh-hour bargaining compromise, I suggested $5.05 for allowance and a written guarantee on labor's part to do dishes every Tuesday.

(*Confidently.*)

I knew that this offer would bridge our differences. And you know what happened?

(*Stunned.*)

Management got up, left the bargaining table and told me to go to my room! I couldn't believe it. How much more reasonable do you want a kid to be?

(*Lights fade.*)

UNEQUALIBRIUM
BY ALEXANDER LYRAS AND ROBERT MCCASKILL

A young man, ISAAC, *has a complicated good-night phone call with his girlfriend, Kassandra.* HE *wears sweatpants rolled up to his knees, a synthetic orange tank top, socks, and wool slippers, holds a phone with a long cord stretched across the apartment to his ear.*

SCENE
ISAAC*'s apartment. Scattered about the stage, ski pants, sweatshirt, a thick flannel shirt, duck boots, running shoes, ski goggles, a wool hat, a long winter coat, a warm-up pullover with gloves in the front pouch, a CD Walkman, keys, and a small cardboard box overstuffed with office supplies.*

TIME
Friday night and Saturday, December 14 and 15, 2001

DISENTANGLED

ISAAC: Good-bye! It's late. I'm tired! You're great! Good-bye. I'm not mad! No, I'm not coming over tonight, Kassandra.—I'm NOT coming over. Kassandra? Kassandra? Kassandra? Why are you torturing me? I'm NOT mad! Can you hold one sec?

(ISAAC *puts the phone on hold.* HE *walks to a box and pulls out a nine iron.* HE *smashes a small cardboard box to death with it. Feels better. Returns to phone and picks it up.*)

I'm back. Fine, I'm mad! I'm FURIOUS AT YOU!—Because it was our friend's recital, our FRIEND! And you're talking and you're whispering, and you're *Fftffk!* during the performance, like you're in a bar! And I tell you to *shhh* and you SHHH me back LOUDER! That face you make! The whole thing was interrupted! And you're with ME, Kass, PEOPLE KNOW YOU.

Everyone's a potential client at this point, a very needed client, you know that. The LAST thing I need at this point is to lose a design because my girlfriend's being a cunt.—Hello?

(HE *hangs up.*)

I gotta watch my fucking language now?

(HE *redials.*)

Trouble in paradise. Hi. . . . It slipped! I'm sorry. I promise I will never use that word again. I promise!—Okay . . . I'll come over.

(ISAAC *puts both duck boots on.*)

Yes, now I'm putting my Timberlands on. You know, can I just say that you are my greatest joy and the only source of misery in my life.

Well, why are you being like this now? I need you to be supportive right now and you're on a rampage!

(HE *puts the flannel shirt on, accidentally buttoning it over the phone cord.*)

I AM trying to! What do you think I'm doing every day? The market's not what it used to be, darling, and right now web masters are a notch below typewriter repairmen!

I can't answer that.—No, because, there is no answer, okay? There is no SYSTEM for figuring this out. You can live your life like you think there is—like the corporate winners who downsized me—but it's a lie. Because the truth is: NOBODY KNOWS ANYTHING.

I'm putting my jacket on!

(ISAAC *puts on the winter jacket. Notices the phone cord in his shirt. Pulls it out.*)

These people? These corporate people are all scared to DEATH to take a gamble!

(ISAAC *begins to search for something. Pulls stuff from pockets. Shakes out the clothes and shoes on the floor.*)

Their entire philosophy of life is predicated upon the idea of RISK AVERSION.

God, if I hear that term again I'm gonna put my fist through a shower curtain. These people can't take a piss without figuring out if it's risk averse or not. And all the MBAs and LMMs and whatever other initials I don't have that they get a salary in perpetuity for are nothing more than a form of insurance, it's all insurance!

(ISAAC *searches elsewhere on the set.*)

—I'm trying to find my keys, Kass. When I do, I'll walk out the door! You're like them, you realize that? Demand! That's what they do. They demand that big money-making idea! But make a mistake and you're fired. These people will never understand that mistakes are the only time anything interesting ever happens.

You know what these people gave me after six years and four months of work for them, Kass? Know what they gave me? A cardboard box with my belongings in it.

(ISAAC *searches underneath the beaten cardboard box.*)

—I'm not *indicting* anyone! I'm saying I have to reinvent everything from scratch now, on my own, with no help and therefore I have a different form of stress, WHICH YOU ARE NOW EXACERBATING!

(HE *finds the keys!*)

No, I'm NOT coming over! 'Cause I'm not waiting forty minutes for the F train, that's why!

(HE *takes off duck boots and winter jacket.*)

—I can't afford a taxi to BROOKLYN, Kassandra. You want to hear me say it? I CAN'T AFFORD THAT.

(*Rips off flannel shirt.*)

This isn't about what I want, I asked what YOU want! That's how we started this however many years ago — Fine, you wanna know what I want? I want to stop you mid-mood swing, 'cause I have problems too. I want my severance check without having to sue somebody. I want the other five hundred thousand losers who got laid off to stay out of MY Starbucks 'cause I can't get a seat. I never wanna have to eat at Gray's Papaya again. — I want a break! I want a break FROM ABOVE 'cause I deserve it! And if I don't get it right this second — NOPE, DIDN'T GET IT! — Then

RIGHT NOW what I want to do is to go for a long run and get all this hostility out.

(*Pulls jogging sweatshirt on backwards and inside out.*)

—I know it's snowing out, I like to run in the snow.

(*Fixes sweatshirt.*)

—Where do you get that from what I said?—So I'm subconsciously running away from you? I run when I'm stressed, that means we're breaking up?!

(*Puts on running shoes and all-weather pants. The phone cord, between his legs, gets wrapped into his pants without him realizing it.*)

Okay, I'm gonna say something now, I don't want you to get mad. No more Ricki Lake. No more. Because you get this swivel-chair psychology and honestly—(*Laugh.*) I have no place to put it.

(He *paces with phone cord caught inside his pants.*)

—Okay, Kassi, don't start that! Kassandra, Kassandra, Kassandra. . . . Stop crying.

Kass? Kassi? Please don't cry.—Shmushy? Who's a mushy? Who am I gonna smush with?

If I come over, you'll stop crying? Yes, I'll come over.

(*Pulls off sweatshirt and running shoes, puts on duck boots.*)

—I AM serious about us! Do you really think we would have combined CDs if I wasn't serious?

Go, if you have a suggestion, we're communicating here.

(*Puts on flannel.*)

—What about my ego?—Well, whose ego *should* I worry about, darling, my fellow man? I refuse to help my fellow man, my fellow man just LAID ME— I'm sorry, did I interrupt you? Egomaniacal? It's egoMANIACAL now?

(*Takes off flannel. Puts on one running shoe.*)

—Uhuh, well . . . the only part of you that's grown in the past four years is your ability to fight. I'm convinced you need to feel pain! I'm convinced you like it. HEY, MAYBE I COULD START SMACKING YOU AROUND LIKE YOUR FATHER DID, HOW'S THAT SOUND?!

—Hello?

(He *hangs up.*)

Oh, that was a genius move. *Smacking you around like your father did?*

Why don't you just offer to dig her mother up from the grave while you're at it?

(He *redials.*)

—I feel terrible for saying that. That was unfair for me to say. Please pick up the phone. Pleeeease?

—HI! That was way outta line for me to say. I didn't mean that. That's not what I meant!—What? Don't say that.

(Hops around with one shoe, one boot. Puts jacket over tank top.)

—Okay, I'm coming over. I'm coming right now! I'll take a cab. I'll run down to the Garden and hire a limo!—Kass, don't do it! Because you've been dry for two years, don't throw it away.

I DIDN'T MEAN IT, I JUST SAID—WHY DO YOU PUT WORDS IN MY MOUTH! BUT YOU KNOW THAT'S NOT WHAT I MEANT, CYNTHIA! I mean Kassandra!

—Hello?

FUCK ME!

(He *hangs up.*)

Kassandra. . . . Your girlfriend's name is Kassandra.

(He *redials.*)

That was an accident. I didn't mean Kassandra—Cynthia!. . . I meant Kassandra. Please pick up the phone?

Hi. . . . Because you're reminding me of her right now.—Because Cynthia had no context for the world outside of her own emotions. The only thing that didn't bore her was her!

That IS why I'm with you! Oh, my god! You've had an impact on my life, Okay! I'm dented!

Why are you acting so irrational? Yes, you are! Is it that time of month, did your dream catcher fall, what?!

You're gonna blame this on the pill again? You're gonna blame this on the pill? THEN STOP TAKING IT!—You did? When?—

What does that mean?—I don't understand, every other day, every other day is not how that works. It's every day, Kassi. Everything in this world is every day. Are you pregnant? Well, don't you think you should check?

I don't under—you telling me you're fucking someone else? Are you FUCKING someone else? *Blawawawa? Waum um* what? You're gonna stutter on that response? Okay, you know. Don't answer. Now I'm DEFINITELY not coming over!

(He *attempts to put the running shoes on. Gets entangled again in the phone cord.*)

No, hang up, I won't call back! I'm putting *Rage Against the Machine* in my Walkman and running straight to fucking Chappaqua and you won't have to worry about it 'cause you'll never be close enough to hurt me again.

(He *hangs up. Puts on full running gear.*)

Good! I'm free. I can finally have sex with other women. Yes! I'm gonna get so laid! That Asian girl in 2B is definitely gonna hear from me.

(He *clears the stage of everything. Sits. Thinks. Has a nervous break-down. Cries. Heads to phone. Redials.*)

Oh, pick up the phone, Kassandra. PICK UP THE PHONE AND ACT LIKE A, A—WOMAN!

HI . . . I have one last question for you: Will you marry me?—I am nothing but real. Will you marry me?—It's not because you're pregnant, well maybe it is, I just wanna start a home with you.

Here's what I propose to do. It's sixty-four blocks to your place, I'm gonna run there. And when I get there and propose in person, I will hear my answer. — Don't say anything, I'm out the door!

. . . What?

PLAY SOURCES AND ACKNOWLEDGMENTS

Auburn, David, © 2002. (*Fifth Planet and Other Plays*). *We Had a Very Good Time*. Reprinted by permission of the author. Contact Chris Till, Paradigm, 19 W. 44th St., Suite 1410, New York, NY 10036.

Baitz, Jon Robin, © 2006. *The Paris Letter*. Reprinted by permission of the author. Please direct inquiries to Creative Artists Agency, 162 Fifth Ave., 6th floor, New York, NY 10010.

Basham, Rebecca, © 2007. *Imagine*. Reprinted by permission of the author. Contact Rebecca Basham, 11 Morningside Drive, Trenton, NJ 08618.

Bates, Brendon William, © 2005. *Corps Values*. Amateurs and professionals are hereby warned that this excerpt and *Corps Values* is fully protected by copyright law and subject to royalty. All rights in all current and future media are strictly reserved. No part of this work may be used for any purpose without the written consent of the author. All inquiries concerning production, publication, or reprinting, or use of this work in any form should be addressed to the author: Brendon William Bates, c/o The New York Theatre Experience, Inc., PO Box 1606, Murray Hill Station, New York, NY 10156.

Beckim, Chad, © 2007. *'Nami*. Please direct queries to Chad Beckim, c/o The New York Theatre Experience's Plays & Playwrights, PO Box 1606, Murray Hill Station, New York, NY 10156.

Blank, Jessica and Erik Jensen, © 2004. *The Exonerated*. All rights reserved. Excerpt reprinted by permission of Faber and Faber and Farrar, Inc, an affiliate of Farrar, Straus, and Giroux, LLC, 19 Union Square West, New York, NY 10003.

Bragen, Andy, © 2007. *Heirloom*. Reprinted by permission of the author. For queries visit his website (www.andybragen.com) or contact agent Mark Orsini, Bret Adams Ltd., 448 West 44th St., New York, NY 10036; 212-765-5630; morsini@bretadamsltd.com.

McCormack, Thomas, © 2007. *Storytellers*. Reprinted by permission of the author. The selection quoted from the play is called "Why I Quit Philosophy." Direct inquiries by email to: cheerskep@aol.com.

McDonagh, Martin, © 2003. *The Pillowman*. All rights reserved. Excerpt reprinted by permission of Faber and Faber and Farrar, Inc, an affiliate of Farrar, Straus, and Giroux, LLC, 19 Union Square West, New York, NY 10003.

McDonald, Heather, © 2002. *An Almost Holy Picture*. Reprinted by permission of the author. Please direct inquiries to the Peregrine Whittlesey Agency, 279 Central Park West, New York, NY 10024; 212-787-1802.

McIlvain, Josh, © 2006. *The Boss's Daughter*. Reprinted by permission of the author. Please direct all queries to joshmcilvain@yahoo.com.

McNally, Terrence, © 2006. *Dedication or The Stuff of Dreams*. Used by permission of Grove/Atlantic Inc.; www.groveatlantic.com.

Malpede, Karen, © 2007. *Prophecy*. Reprinted by permission of the author. All rights reserved. Inquiries should be made to Barbara Hogenson, The Barbara Hogenson Agency, Inc., 165 West End Ave., Suite 19-C; New York, NY 10023; Tel: 212-874-8084; email: bhogenson@aol.com.

Mason, Clifford, © 2000. *O.T. Fairclough and Roger Mais*. Reprinted by permission of the author. Inquiries should be made to Clifford Mason at clm532@earthlink.net; 212-769-9606.

Mee, Charles, © 2000. *Big Love*. Reprinted by permission of the author. All rights reserved. Charles Mee's plays are on his website at www.charlesmee.org. No need to contact the author if doing the monologue; for full productions, contact Thomas Pearson at ICM. Tel: 212-556-5600; tpearson@icmtalent.com.

Mee, Charles, © 2005. *Fêtes de la Nuit*. All rights reserved. Reprinted by permission of the author. Charles Mee's plays are on his website at www.charlesmee.org. No need to contact the author if doing the monologue; for full productions, contact Thomas Pearson at ICM. Tel: 212-556-5600; tpearson@icmtalent.com.

Miller, Tim, © 2002. *The Proposal*. Reprinted by permission of the author, whose book *1001 Beds* earned the 2007 Lamda Literary Foundation Award for best book in Drama-Theater. Miller can be reached at his website: http://hometown.aol.com/millertale. Read his blog: http://timmillerperfomer.blogspot.com.

Soland, Lisa, © 2003. *The Rebirth*. Reprinted by permission of the author. Please direct inquiries to Lisa Soland, PO Box 33081, Granada Hills, CA 91394, or lisasoland@aol.com.

Soland, Lisa © 1991. *Red Roses*. Reprinted by permission of the author. Please direct inquiries to Lisa Soland, PO Box 33081, Granada Hills, CA 91394, or lisasoland@aol.com.

Spitz, Marc, © 2001. *Shyness Is Nice*. Reprinted courtesy of the author and the Carol Mann Agency, 55 5th Ave., New York, NY 10003.

Swedeen, Staci, © 2007. *Catch & Release*. Reprinted by permission of the author. Please direct inquiries to Elaine Devlin Literary Agency, c/o Plus Entertainment, 20 West 23 St., 3rd Floor, New York, NY 10010, or to the author: staciswede@aol.com or www.staciswedeen.com.

Temperley, Stephen, © 2004. *The Pilgrim Papers*. All rights reserved. Reprinted by permission of the author. Please direct inquiries concerning rights to Bret Adams, Ltd., 448 West 44th St., New York, NY 10036; 212-765-5630.

Temperley, Stephen, © 2003. *Souvenir*. All rights reserved. Reprinted by permission of the author. Please direct inquiries concerning rights to Dramatists Play Service, 440 Park Avenue South, New York, NY 10016; 212-683-8960.

van Itallie, Jean-Claude, © 2005. *Fear Itself, Secrets of the White House*. Reprinted by permission of the author. Visit his website: www.vanitallie.com. Inquiries: Morgan Jenness, Abrams Artists, 275 Seventh Avenue, New York, NY 10001; 646-486-4600.

van Itallie, Jean-Claude, © 2004. *Light*. Reprinted by permission of the author. Visit his website: www.vanitallie.com. Inquiries: Morgan Jenness, Abrams Artists, 275 Seventh Avenue, New York, NY 10001; 646-486-4600.

Wellman, Mac, © 2002. *Bitter Bierce*. Reprinted by permission of the author. For this and other Wellman titles and information contact: Playscripts, Inc., 325 West 38th Street, Suite 305, New York, NY 10018; Toll-Free Phone: 1-866-NEW-PLAY (1-866-639-7529); email: info@playscripts.com.

Wilson, August, © 2003, 2006. *Gem of the Ocean*. The Play is published by and reprinted with the permission of Theatre Communications Group, 520 Eighth Avenue, New York, NY 10018.

Winter, Gary, © 2004. *At Said*. Reprinted by permission of the author. Inquiries concerning all rights should be made to: Gary Winter, 195 Willoughby Avenue, #402, Brooklyn, NY 11205; gary.winter@nyu.edu.

Additionally, the editors would like to thank the extraordinary writers who so graciously allowed their work to be used in this volume, as well as: Applause Books, Kathleen Ausman, Beth Blickers, Carol Mann Agency, Justin Cavin, Clare Cerullo, June Clark, Margie Connor, Colleen Coyne, Rochelle and Martin Denton, the Drama Book Shop, Peter Filichia, Carol Flannery, Kenneth Ferrone, Victoria Fox, Peter Franklin, Gary Garrison, Tracy Gibbons, Seth Glewen, Pam Green, Corinne Hayoun, Patrick Herold, Linda Konner, Morgan Jenness, Jonathan Lomma, Matthew Love, Eric Lupfer, Bernadette Malavarca, Michael Messina, Barry Moss, Nancy Nelson and Randy Lanchner, Mark Orsini, Kathleen Peirce, Jonathan Rand, Random House, Peter Rubie, Kathleen Russo, Jessica Sarbo, Will Scherlin, Karen Schimmel, Marit Shuman, the Shuman and Nolan families, Rita Battat Silverman and Steve Silverman, Keith Strunk, Ursinus College, Kathleen Warnock, Stephanie Weir, Peregrine Whittlesey, and Gary Winter.

THE EDITORS

Joyce E. Henry, Ph.D., is professor emerita of Theatre and Communication Studies at Ursinus College. She is the editor of *The Wisdom of Shakespeare* and author of *Beat the Bard*. She lives in Collegeville, Pennsylvania.

Rebecca Dunn Jaroff, Ph.D., is assistant professor of English at Ursinus College where she teaches American literature, drama, and journalism. She is the author of several essays on nineteenth-century American women playwrights. She lives in Conshohocken, Pennsylvania.

Bob Shuman, M.F.A., is the owner of Marit Literary Agency in New York. He is an editor, playwright, college professor, composer, and co-author of *Simply Elegant Flowers with Michael George*. A Fellow of the Lark Theatre Company, Bob received Hunter College's Irv Zarkower Award for excellence in playwriting. He lives in New York City.